Sounding the Trumpet

Sounding the Trumpet

The Making of
John F. Kennedy's Inaugural Address

RICHARD J. TOFEL

IVAN R. DEE
Chicago 2005

www.ivanrdee.com

Library of Congress Cataloging-in-Publication Data:
Tofel, Richard J., 1957–
 Sounding the trumpet : the making of John F. Kennedy's inaugural address / Richard J. Tofel.
     p. cm.
 Includes bibliographical references and index.
 ISBN 1-56663-610-8 (cloth : alk. paper)
 1. Kennedy, John F. (John Fitzgerald), 1917–1963—Inauguration, 1961. 2. Presidents—United States—Inaugural addresses. 3. United States—Politics and government—1961–1963. I. Title.
  J82.D91T64 2005
  352.23'86'0973—dc22

                                    2005003804

In memory of Dick Neustadt,
scholar, teacher, mentor, friend

Preface

ONE LEADING contemporary observer called it the finest American political document in more than forty years. Another said it was the best expression of the American spirit since Woodrow Wilson, and perhaps since Emerson. Approaching a half-century after its delivery, it is the source of four separate citations in *Bartlett's Familiar Quotations*, amounting to one-seventh of its entire text. A scholarly study ranked it as the second-greatest American speech of the twentieth century. No matter their politics, historians agree that there is at least one way in which John F. Kennedy ranks with Jefferson, Lincoln, and Franklin Roosevelt— in the quality of his inaugural address.

This book attempts to understand the enduring appeal of Kennedy's inaugural address through a close examination of its origins. I have had the good fortune of the first extensive interviews ever granted on this subject by Theodore C. Sorensen, special counsel to the late president. As will become clear, other than Kennedy himself—who seems never to have discussed the origins of the speech—Sorensen is in the best position to describe how the speech evolved and why it contained the words that it did. In addition, this book reproduces the key source material, the surviving drafts of the speech and a few important related papers, in seven appendices. None of these documents, save the text of the inaugural address as delivered, has ever before been published in full; two—one handwritten, one in shorthand—have never before been transcribed in full for publication.

The approach of the narrative is relatively straightforward. We begin by setting the scene of Kennedy's inauguration, placing the words the new president spoke on January 20, 1961, in the moment of their delivery. Then we go back to describe the process, the craftsmanship and collaboration that brought those words into the world. This is done first chronologically ("when"), then contextually ("why"), and finally textually ("how"), literally paragraph by paragraph. On all three levels, the story that emerges is surprising, not at all the standard version found in textbooks or even recent biographies.

Finally, the impact of the speech is charted over the now more than forty years since President Kennedy's assassination. What emerges, I believe, is a clearer picture of why Kennedy's memory continues to exert such an emotional tug on a country in which a significant majority of the population was born well after his death. That appeal may even be growing as we once again face a "powerful challenge" and find that the "same revolutionary beliefs for which our forebears fought" have been "placed at issue around the globe." As I hope this book helps to explain, the essence of Kennedy's appeal lies in these words.

Contents

"*Unhestitatingly I should put him down as the best talker I have ever known, one whose talk was not a brilliant monologue or a string of epigrams, but a communal effort which quickened and elevated the whole discussion and brought out the best of other people.*"

—John Buchan, *Pilgrim's Way*

Sounding the Trumpet

Part One

January 20

The president-elect of the United States began his work-day in the bathtub. He had arrived home at nearly four o'clock in the morning, following a night of parties, but was awake again just after eight.

The 7.7 inches of snow that had fallen on Washington the previous afternoon and evening had compelled his personal secretary, Mrs. Evelyn Lincoln, to spend the night in a spare bedroom in his Georgetown townhouse. Hearing her stirring, he appeared at the bedroom door and asked for the reading copy of his speech. As Mrs. Lincoln ate her breakfast, she heard him in the bath, reading the speech aloud.

He continued to practice as he dressed for church, and in between bites as he ate his own customary breakfast—a large orange juice, two poached eggs, three strips of crisp bacon, and coffee with cream and sugar—in the downstairs living room. When he was finished eating, Mrs. Lincoln came in and gave him the daily allocation of pills for his adrenal insufficiency and chronic back pain. As the historian Robert Dallek notes, these would have included an extra dose of steroids to enhance his performance later in the day. Since what he regarded as a disappointing performance when he had accepted the Democratic presidential nomination in Los Angeles the previous July, John F. Kennedy had opted for additional steroids on the days of major speeches. On the occasion of his inaugural, he may also have earlier had an injection of Dexedrine, a stimulant, from his personal physician, Dr. Janet Travell.

The day before, Thursday, January 19, 1961, had been one of anticipation and pageantry—and also of near chaos.

At nine o'clock in the morning, for the second time in the seventy-two days since his election as president by a margin of just one-tenth of 1 percent of the popular vote over Republican Vice President Richard Nixon, Kennedy had met at the White House with President Dwight Eisenhower. The two leaders had been joined by their secretaries of state, treasury, and defense. Eisenhower had harbored doubts about Kennedy's seriousness of purpose and readiness for the presidency, but Kennedy was growing on him, impressing him with his command of facts and arguments. Both men delighted in Eisenhower's demonstration of how quickly the president could summon a helicopter to the White House lawn. Eisenhower ended the visit by inviting the Kennedys to come by the White House the next morning earlier than previously planned for a cup of coffee before the ride to the Capitol to take the oath of office. It was a marked improvement from the last transition, eight years earlier, when Eisenhower and Harry Truman had barely spoken.

Kennedy—temporarily evicted from his own N Street townhouse as his wife Jacqueline organized the family's move to new quarters—returned to the P Street home of his friend, the artist Bill Walton, for a series of meetings, and then went on to afternoon receptions at two Washington hotels. But around him, all that almost everyone could talk about was the snow.

It began around noon, soon covering the green paint freshly applied to the lawn surrounding the Lincoln Memorial and the "Roost-No-More" applied to tree branches on the next day's parade route to deter starlings. The plane carrying former President Herbert Hoover to the inauguration circled the Washington airport for an hour before turning back to Miami. Hoover was a friend of Kennedy patriarch Joseph Kennedy, Sr., who had been a member of the Hoover Commission on government reorganization. At Kennedy Sr.'s request, the former president had brokered the meeting of candidates Kennedy and Nixon the Monday after the 1960 presidential election, at which Nixon made clear he would not contest the outcome. Now Hoover spent nine hours aloft, and missed the next day's ceremony.

Back on the ground in Washington, as the afternoon rush hour ground to a halt in the storm, 115 cars were abandoned on the George Washington Parkway. Some Eisenhower White House staffers were compelled to spend their final night in office in the basement shelter. The storm actually intensified as it moved north, eventually dropping 12 inches of snow on Philadelphia and 10 inches in New York City (where schools were ordered closed for Friday). Harrisburg, Pennsylvania, was hit with 20 inches, the largest storm in 15 years, and Middletown, New York, recorded 29 inches.

But nearly eight inches was easily enough to bring Washington to its knees. The president-elect and Mrs. Kennedy made it a few blocks down N Street to the home of former New York governor and senator Herbert Lehman for a reception in honor of Eleanor Roosevelt. But where *Washington Post* publisher Philip Graham and his wife Katharine had been expecting six hundred guests at their R Street home for a dinner party, only two hundred made it through, and the Kennedys were not among them.

Hundreds of workers, a number of them military personnel, took to the streets throughout the afternoon and evening to begin the process of shoveling out, and the Secret Service doggedly continued to shuttle the Kennedys to events they felt they simply could not miss. These included an inaugural concert at Constitution Hall and a Democratic National Committee gala organized by Kennedy friend Frank Sinatra at the National Guard Armory, for which six thousand tickets had been sold, raising $1.4 million. The Constitution Hall concert played to a mostly empty auditorium, and the Kennedys left at intermission. Performers at the DNC gala included Leonard Bernstein, Harry Belafonte, Ethel Merman, Ella Fitzgerald, Milton Berle, Nat King Cole, Mahalia Jackson, Juliet Prowse, Bette Davis, Laurence Olivier, Jimmy Durante, Kennedy in-law Peter Lawford, and Sinatra himself. But many of the performers were late in arriving, and the gala's beginning was delayed from nine o'clock in the evening to eleven o'clock; once begun, it dragged on into the early morning.

Jacqueline Kennedy, who had given birth to her second child (by caesarean section) less than two months earlier, returned home from the gala around midnight. But her husband plowed on, moving to a party thrown by his father at Paul Young's restaurant. Finding aides Kenneth O'Donnell and Dave Powers at that party sipping champagne with their wives, JFK was clearly jealous. He told them, "You two are living like Presidents tonight. I suppose you'll be laughing it up here for another three hours after I go home and get into bed with my inaugural address."

Even in the wee hours of the morning, the speech was on his mind. He had had the final draft at his side for nearly a full day. Walton later recalled that when he pointed out the text of Jefferson's inaugural, reproduced in the program for the Constitution Hall concert, Kennedy had told him, "It's better than mine." But even if this tale is not apocryphal, it would have been a bit of false modesty. Knowing that he would be overheard by Hugh Sidey of *Time* magazine, Kennedy had told Theodore Sorensen, "It will be a sensation." And when *New York Herald Tribune* reporter Marguerite Higgins later asked him at the more relaxed gala if he had a good speech, Kennedy told her, "It's a smash."

Just before nine o'clock the next morning, Kennedy left his home, accompanied by his friend Walton, to attend Friday mass at Holy Trinity Roman Catholic Church in Georgetown. This delighted his mother, who had been sitting quietly waiting for the service to begin, and had not expected him. After mass, he stopped by the home of N Street neighbors Charles Montgomery and his daughter Helen, who had often hosted reporters assigned to stake out the Kennedy townhouse during the transition, and gave the Montgomerys a plaque from the journalists in appreciation of their hospitality. Then it was home again to change into formal attire for the inauguration. The car to take the Kennedys to the White House arrived just before eleven o'clock; House Speaker Sam Rayburn and Inaugural Committee Chairman Senator John Sparkman of Alabama rode along with the incoming president and first lady.

At the White House, coffee was quickly served and removed, and the two presidents left together for the Capitol just after 11:30, in accord with a tradition in place since 1837. Eisenhower had followed Kennedy's request that top hats replace homburgs as the fashion of the day.* As Ike put on his top hat, Mamie Eisenhower said, "He looks just like Paddy the Irishman."

ↄ Like all inaugurations, it was a day of firsts, and other superlatives.

*Spotting *New York Times* reporter Bill Lawrence in a homburg that morning, Kennedy quipped, "There is always some bastard that doesn't get the word."

At forty-three, Kennedy had become the youngest man ever elected to the office; his wife was just thirty-one. He was the first president born in the twentieth century and had already named to his young cabinet only one man born in the nineteenth. Eisenhower, at seventy, was the oldest president in the nation's history.* Beyond Eisenhower, the entire cohort brought to power in the wake of the Second World War was aging. Harold Macmillan of Great Britain and Nikita Khrushchev of the Soviet Union were each sixty-six, while China's Mao Zedong was sixty-seven. Jawaharlal Nehru of India was seventy-one, David Ben-Gurion of Israel seventy-four, and Konrad Adenauer of West Germany eighty-five. Kennedy—only the second man to assume the presidency during the lifetime of both his parents (his father was seventy-two)—truly did represent a new generation.†

After thirty years of frumpiness from Eleanor Roosevelt, Bess Truman, and Mamie Eisenhower, Jacqueline Kennedy was a sensation. For the inauguration she wore a dress from Bergdorf's, a wool coat with sable collar and matching muff designed by Oleg Cassini, and a Halston pillbox hat. Halston later recalled,

> . . . it was very windy and when she stepped out of the limo she put up her hand to the pillbox to keep it from flying away.

---

*Theodore Roosevelt had been forty-two when he became president after the assassination of William McKinley, but was forty-six by the time he was elected in his own right. Kennedy's youth relative to past presidents has been somewhat exaggerated, however. Six of Kennedy's thirty-three predecessors had taken office in their forties: James Polk, Franklin Pierce, and James Garfield were all forty-nine; Grover Cleveland was forty-seven; and Ulysses Grant was forty-six. Two first ladies had been younger than Jacqueline Kennedy: Julia Tyler (twenty-four) and Frances Cleveland (twenty-one). But both Tyler and Cleveland had married previously widowed presidents (and both had done so well into their husband's terms of office).

†George W. Bush was the third president to have both parents living at the time he came to office. Ulysses Grant was the first.

She put a slight dent in the hat. The dent appeared in every photograph. Women started putting dents in their pillboxes and designers even started designing them that way.

John Kennedy was the first sitting senator to become president since Warren Harding, and only the second such senator in history. The last Democratic senator before him nominated for the presidency had been Stephen Douglas, who lost to Abraham Lincoln a hundred years earlier. Kennedy was also the first president since Andrew Johnson, Lincoln's successor, to bring to the White House experience in both the House and the Senate. Less auspiciously, he was also the first president in the twentieth century to recapture the White House for his party while losing seats in the Congress.

Most significant in 1960–1961, John Kennedy was to be the first Roman Catholic president. Before Kennedy, only one Catholic had ever been nominated for president by a major party—Governor Al Smith of New York by the Democrats in 1928. Smith had lost badly to Herbert Hoover, failing even to carry his own home state, a victim of Coolidge prosperity and support for Prohibition (which he opposed), but also, clearly, of prejudice. He had said bitterly after the campaign that "the time hasn't come when a man can say his beads in the White House."

Thirty-two years later it was still not clear whether the time had come. A 1956 Gallup Poll showed that 22 percent of voters admitted they would not vote even for a well-qualified Catholic nominated by their own party. Religion was the dominant issue in Kennedy's 1960 primary contests with Hubert Humphrey in Wisconsin and then West Virginia. Even when Kennedy won those rounds, with overwhelmingly Protestant West Virginia the key showdown, he felt compelled in September to address questions of his private faith and public responsibilities in a major speech to the Greater Houston Ministerial Association, and then to take often pointed questions from the clergymen.

After all of that, one of Kennedy's top political advisers still estimated that the candidate's Catholicism may have cost him the five states of California, Montana, New Hampshire, Ohio, and Wisconsin in the general election. Yet Kennedy was not above using his faith to political advantage. He had aides argue in 1956, albeit unsuccessfully, that it was a reason to put him on the national ticket. In 1960, by the same estimate cited earlier, fellow Catholics voting their faith over their politics may have provided the margin of victory in the five states of Massachusetts, Michigan, Minnesota, Pennsylvania, and Rhode Island. In all, 83 electoral votes gained (out of 303 won)—and 83 lost (out of 219).

ᔥ No matter how many precedents were being broken, the setting for the inauguration was entirely traditional. The ceremony was held on a platform constructed on the East Portico of the Capitol. The first inauguration held on the site had been Andrew Jackson's first, in 1829—only the third such celebration held outdoors. (The first outdoor ceremony, in 1817, had been necessitated when House Speaker Henry Clay refused to permit the plush and undemocratic chairs of senators to blot his chamber, even for a day.) Jackson's second inaugural was held indoors, in the House of Representatives chamber. But in the following 128 years the East Portico became the setting for every presidential inauguration save two—William Howard Taft's, in 1909, forced indoors by a winter storm, and Franklin Roosevelt's fourth and final oath-taking, in 1945, which took place during a quiet wartime ceremony at the White House. At least three times before, at Ulysses Grant's second inaugural in 1873, James Garfield's in 1881, and Grover Cleveland's second in 1893, outdoor inaugurals had gone forward in the snow; at dawn on the day of Grant's 1873 ceremony, the temperature in Washington was four degrees below zero.

The ceremonies this day began shortly after noon as President Eisenhower and Vice President Nixon, top hats held over their hearts, descended the steps of the East Portico to the strains of "Hail to the Chief" from the Marine Corps band. Technically, John Kennedy had already been president for nine minutes. Eisenhower and Nixon were followed by Vice President–elect Lyndon Johnson and Senator (and 1952 Democratic vice-presidential nominee) Sparkman. Johnson and Sparkman carried their overcoats, but, once in the air, quickly put them on. It was twenty-two degrees, with a wind blowing from the northwest at eighteen miles per hour. (In more modern parlance, that yields a "wind chill" of just eight degrees above zero.) As the guests arrived at their chairs they found a grey blanket, for protection against the cold, draped over its back. The blankets were marked "USN— Naval Station."

President-elect Kennedy entered next, greeted by "Ruffles and Flourishes" and then Sousa's "Washington Post March."

Seated in the platform's front row this day were five presidents and first ladies, past, present, and future. Collectively the men were those who held the office over a period of nearly thirty years, from 1945 to 1974. Beginning at the audience's left came Pat Nixon, then Mamie Eisenhower, Lady Bird Johnson, Jacqueline Kennedy, Dwight Eisenhower, and John Kennedy. To the right of the podium sat Lyndon Johnson, Richard Nixon, Senator Sparkman, and Harry and Bess Truman. Two widowed former first ladies were also present: Edith Wilson, seated just behind, and Eleanor Roosevelt, with the diplomatic corps.

Nearly all but the Kennedys brought mixed emotions to the event. The Eisenhowers were on their way out, the general's heir apparent having been rejected by the voters. The Nixons, of course, took that defeat even more personally. Nixon's eight years as vice president made him more experienced than Kennedy, and he had the edge in seriousness as well, even if not in likeability. (Moreover, while he denied it, Nixon would have been entitled to blame his defeat to some extent on the sometimes tepid nature of Eisenhower's support in the campaign.) Johnson, too, had been bested by Kennedy for this spot, at the Democratic Convention. Eleanor Roosevelt had favored Adlai Stevenson, the Democratic standard-bearer in 1952 and 1956, for a third nomination; she still resented public criticism from Kennedy's father many years earlier, considered John Kennedy immature, and had faulted him for not opposing Senator Joseph McCarthy with sufficient vigor during Kennedy's first two years in the Senate. The presidency, she had said in a pointed reference to Kennedy's book *Profiles in Courage*, was no place for "someone who understands what courage is and admires it, but has not quite the independence to have it."

Harry Truman had bitterly attacked Kennedy just days before the Democratic Convention opened, calling the gathering a "pre-arranged . . . mockery . . . controlled by one . . . candidate" and chiding Kennedy personally:

> Senator, are you certain that you are quite ready for the country, or that the country is ready for you in the role of President . . .? We need a man with the greatest possible maturity and experience. . . . May I urge you to be patient?

Kennedy had replied in kind, "Mr. Truman regards an open convention as one which studies all the candidates, reviews their records, and then takes his advice." This rift had since healed somewhat, and Truman had a date for the following day to visit

Kennedy in the White House. It would be his first time in the building since he and Bess had moved out eight years before.

Still, Kennedy had just told CBS correspondent Nancy Hanschman (later Dickerson)—a woman he had once dated—that "he wasn't half as surprised to be President as a lot of people were to see him there." In all, 105 invited guests were scheduled to be seated on the main platform—16 of them members of the Kennedy family, the least surprised of the assemblage. When the new president reached his chair, he was again greeted by his predecessor. The ceremony was supposed to begin immediately, but not enough seating had been provided for all the guests, and a six-minute delay ensued while additional chairs were located and brought out. Kennedy and Eisenhower discussed Cornelius Ryan's new book, *The Longest Day*, the story of D day, Eisenhower's moment of triumph nearly seventeen years earlier.

"Fairly far up" in one of the higher rows, off the main platform, sat Theodore Sorensen, designated as special counsel to the president in the new administration. Sorensen, separated from his wife, was accompanied by his sister Ruth. He had already served Kennedy for eight years, beginning at the age of twenty-four. He had joined Kennedy just after his election to the Senate, following an eight-month stint on the Temporary Committee of the Congress on Railroad Retirement Legislation and earlier work at the Federal Security Agency, the forerunner of Eisenhower's Department of Health, Education and Welfare. On the side, he had published articles in such liberal publications as *The New Republic* and *The Progressive*. On the day he went to work for the senator from Massachusetts, Sorensen had never set foot in New England. Eight years later he still had never been overseas. A Lincoln, Nebraska, Unitarian by birth, a second-generation George Norris progressive by inheritance and conviction, and a lawyer by training, Sorensen soon was Kennedy's top legislative policy aide, a role he continued to play. Kennedy called Sorensen "my intellectual blood bank." Others used a different sanguinary metaphor: "When Jack is wounded, Ted bleeds."

In addition, for more than four years, since Kennedy's abortive attempt to gain the 1956 Democratic vice-presidential nomination at that year's convention in Chicago, Sorensen had worked nearly full time on the Kennedy presidential campaign. Beyond that, Sorensen had become Kennedy's preferred collaborator in crafting his writings and speeches, from Senate and campaign addresses to magazine articles to position papers to *Profiles in Courage*, published in 1956. Michael Medved has written that "Sorensen gave Kennedy the power of words." Kennedy told Tip O'Neill, his successor in the House of Representatives, that "I never had anyone who could write for me until Ted came along." Sorensen himself later wrote that,

> As the years went on, and I came to know what he thought on each subject as well as how he wished to say it, our standard and style became increasingly one. . . . [W]e tried repeatedly but unsuccessfully to find other wordsmiths who could write for him in the style to which he was accustomed. The style of those whom we tried may have been very good. It may have been superior. But it was not his.

Others put it somewhat differently. Arthur Schlesinger later noted that "Sorensen had come to feel that no one else knew the candidate's mind so well or reproduced his idiom so accurately. Justifiably proud of his special relationship, he tended to resent interlopers."

Ted Sorensen was the person who had told John Kennedy, as he awoke on the morning after the cliff-hanger 1960 election, that, yes, he had won the presidency. Sorensen was the first person, the next day, offered a job in the new Kennedy administration. But there were limits to the relationship, as there seemingly were to all of Kennedy's relationships. The two men, Sorensen later wrote, were "close in a peculiarly impersonal way." "I don't think," he said, "that I ever regarded myself as his equal." In an interview in 1959, Jacqueline Kennedy said, "Ted is such a little boy in so many ways. The way he almost puffs himself up when he talks to Jack. He hero-worships Jack, of course, and I think it was only last year that Ted started calling him 'Jack' and I think he asked Jack first if he could."

The presidential scholar Richard Neustadt, who knew both men, observed that "never have two people been more intimate and more separate." Nevertheless, Sorensen recalls, the morning of January 20, 1961, "was a morning of incredible elation for me—and perhaps the word 'incredible,' or 'incredulous,' should be underlined."

By quarter past twelve all the chairs were in place on the in-augural platform, and Sparkman stepped forward to begin. The Marine band led off the program with "America the Beautiful."

Next came the invocation, delivered by Richard Cardinal Cushing of Boston, favorite prelate of the Kennedy family. In the biting cold, and in a voice at once both stern and singsong, Cushing droned on for more than six hundred words, over seven and a half minutes. As Kennedy later confided to John Kenneth Galbraith, "I knew it would be long, but halfway through I was saved by the thought that here is Kennedy, the first Catholic president, being inaugurated, and [conservative, Republican-leaning New Yorker Francis] Cardinal Spellman is having to watch it on television."

Shortly after Cushing began, smoke started to rise from somewhere inside the podium. The wind quickly blew it clear, but Kennedy, standing closest to the cardinal, was visibly con-cerned. Secret Service chief U. E. Baughman, standing directly behind Eisenhower and Kennedy, summoned a fireman with an extinguisher, and directed one of his agents to locate the source of the smoke. Cushing continued, however, seemingly oblivious; he later said that he feared a bomb and was intent on absorbing the force of the blast. Eisenhower leaned over to Kennedy and whispered, "You must have a hot speech."

After four or five minutes the smoke increased, and Sparkman and Nixon whispered urgently to one another. Baughman three times considered evacuating the wooden platform, from which there was only one narrow exit. As Cushing continued, Kennedy pal Paul ("Red") Fay, seated six or seven rows back, thought the cardinal "went on and on in an endless monotone as though he had been plugged into the wall and wouldn't stop till somebody disconnected him." Meanwhile, four men crawled near and under the podium—two Secret Service agents in overcoats, two firemen in dress uniforms—seeking to determine the source of the smoke and how to stop it. By the time Cushing concluded (and the incoming president made the sign of the cross), the group scrambling around the podium had grown to six; one of the firemen was brandishing the extinguisher. Finally the smoke was traced to a short circuit in the mechanism used to raise and lower the lectern. But the connection was behind a locked panel, and at first it was not clear who had the key. When the right man was located, the panel was unlocked and the device unplugged. After a further two-minute delay, the ceremony continued.

Marian Anderson came forward to sing the "Star-Spangled Banner." Anderson was a black contralto perhaps best known for her 1939 banning from Constitution Hall by the Daughters of the American Revolution, and her subsequent performance, under the sponsorship of Eleanor Roosevelt, of "America the Beautiful" at the Lincoln Memorial. She had also performed at Eisenhower's second inaugural, in 1957. Today, wrote Lincoln Kirstein, "Her laudatory diction made the verse sound like poetry; her mahogany voice was never strained." She opted to sing both verses of the national anthem; reporters observed that, of every-one on the platform, only John Kennedy and vice-presidential daughter Lynda Bird Johnson seemed to know the words to the second verse.

Next came a blessing from Archbishop Iakovos of the Greek Orthodox church. Iakovos was mercifully brief at under three minutes. Kennedy crossed himself again.

At 12:41 P.M., Lyndon Johnson stepped forward to take the vice-presidential oath of office. It was administered by Johnson's mentor, House Speaker Sam Rayburn, with the Bible held by Senate staff aide Franklin Dryden. Johnson flubbed one of his lines: asked by Rayburn to repeat that he took the office "with-out mental reservation or purpose of evasion," Johnson said he took it "without any mental reservation whatever." But LBJ maintained his composure. After the oath-taking he shook hands with Rayburn, Dryden, Nixon, Sparkman, and Kennedy. That made it time for yet another prayer, this one from John-son friend Reverend John Barclay of Central Christian Church in Austin, Texas.

When Barclay concluded, Sparkman introduced the poet Robert Frost, who had been asked by Kennedy to recite some-thing at the inaugural. The president-elect had expressed private concern that Frost might upstage him. The invitation had been extended through Frost's friend Stewart Udall, the incoming sec-retary of the interior. But Kennedy, recalling Edward Everett, had told Udall, "It's a good idea, but we don't want to be like Lincoln at Gettysburg. He is a master of words. We don't want him to steal the show. Let him read a poem." Nevertheless, Kennedy led the applause.

Frost had written a new poem for the occasion, intended as an introduction to an old one. This new work was announced at the time as being entitled "Dedication," and originally consisted of forty-two lines.* But Frost was eighty-six years old, and the sun reflecting off the snow was very bright, even as the wind was rustling his papers. After reciting just six lines, Frost said, "I'm not having a good light here at all. I can't see in this light." Kennedy, presumably embarrassed for the old man, smiled; Jacqueline Kennedy looked stricken. Lyndon Johnson had the presence of mind to jump up and use his top hat to shield Frost's text from the sun. Frost snatched the new vice president's hat, saying, "Here, give me that," to laughter and some applause. But it was immediately clear that the hat would not help enough for Frost to see clearly.

In the years since, Frost's poem has come to be best remembered for its final lines, foretelling

> The glory of a next Augustan age
> Of a power leading from its strength and pride,
> Of a young ambition eager to be tried,
> Firm in our free beliefs without dismay,
> In any game the nations want to play.
> A golden age of poetry and power
> Of which this noonday's the beginning hour.

But in fact these lines were not in the version Frost had intended to read at the inauguration. They were added some days or weeks

---

*As later published, the poem was entitled "For John F. Kennedy His Inauguration: Gift Outright of 'The Gift Outright' (With some preliminary history in rhyme)" and consisted of seventy-seven lines.

later; the full poem was published in a book of Frost poetry in 1962. A near-final version was transmitted from Frost to Kennedy via Interior Secretary Udall on March 1, 1961.

On inauguration day the nation's unofficial poet laureate fell back on a memory untouched by age. He told the crowd, "This was to be a preface to a poem I can say without seeing it. The poem goes like this:

> The land was ours before we were the land's.
> She was our land more than a hundred years
> Before we were her people. She was ours
> In Massachusetts, in Virginia,
> But we were England's, still colonials,
> Possessing what we still were unpossessed by,
> Possessed by what we now no more possessed.
> Something we were withholding made us weak
> Until we found it was ourselves
> We were withholding from our land of living,
> And forthwith found salvation in surrender.
> Such as we were we gave ourselves outright
> (The deed of gift was many deeds of war)
> To the land vaguely realizing westward,
> But still unstoried, artless, unenhanced, . . ."

Now Frost had a twist on the ending of this, "The Gift Outright," first published in 1942. In the original, it concludes, "Such as she was, such as she would become." Today he made it, "Such as she was, such as she has become"—"and for this occasion let me change that to 'what she will become.' And this poem, what I was leading up to, was the dedication of the poem to the President-elect." As the crowd applauded in appreciation and relief, Kennedy warmly thanked Frost and introduced him to Eisenhower.

↶ It was time.

Kennedy, who had been wearing a topcoat throughout the ceremony, removed it quickly, laid it aside, and stood as the band again played "Ruffles and Flourishes." He wore a cutaway with a pearl-colored vest, formal grey trousers with thin black stripes, a white shirt (with a collar borrowed that morning from his father), and a silver checked tie. The top hat he had acquired as a Harvard overseer was left behind at his seat. Beneath his formal wear he had donned thermal underwear against the cold.

The incoming president received a warm smile from Chief Justice Earl Warren. Warren, who had been the Republican governor of California, and that party's 1948 nominee for vice president, had been named chief justice by Eisenhower in 1953, but his leadership of the Supreme Court in civil rights and civil liberties cases had resulted in his estrangement from the GOP. He seemed to welcome the change in administration.

Warren raised his right hand and placed his left hand on the Fitzgerald family Bible, originally purchased by Thomas Fitzgerald, Rose Kennedy's paternal grandfather. The book was a nineteenth-century Douay version, the leading American Catholic Bible since 1825. Sorensen later recalled that Kennedy "sought a family Bible on which he could take the oath of office without arousing the POAU [the anti-Catholic group Protestants and Other Americans United for the Separation of Church and State]."

Thomas Fitzgerald's volume seemed to fit the bill. Kennedy had had the enormous book fetched for the occasion by two Secret Service agents from the attic in the Dorechester home of his mother's brother Tom, the president-elect's godfather. The Bible was held by Supreme Court clerk James Browning.* Kennedy raised his right hand but kept his left at his side as he repeated after the chief justice the oath prescribed by the eighth clause of Article II, Section 1 of the Constitution:

> I, John Fitzgerald Kennedy, do solemnly swear
> that I will faithfully execute the Office of President of the
>   United States,
> and will to the best of my ability,
> preserve, protect and defend the Constitution of the United
>   States.†

Following a tradition begun by George Washington, and prompted by Warren, Kennedy concluded with words not required by the Constitution: "So help me, God." As the crowd applauded, Kennedy shook hands first with Warren, then Johnson, then reached out to Nixon on his left and then to Eisenhower on his right, and turned back to the rostrum to speak. It was eight minutes before one o'clock in the afternoon.

໑ John F. Kennedy had not been known as a great orator. Jack Valenti, watching him speak in 1956, saw a man "plunging ahead with head bowed over the typescript of his speech; our center of attention was the top of his full head of thickly gardened brown hair, since that was the portion of him most visible to his auditors." James MacGregor Burns's 1961 foreword to the paperback

---

*The now-familiar tradition of having the first lady hold the Bible was actually begun by Lady Bird Johnson in 1965.

†The Constitution actually permits a new president to "affirm" if he would prefer not to "swear." Only Franklin Pierce, one of our least successful chief executives, has availed himself of this option. Pierce cited religious objections to the swearing of oaths.

version of his own 1960 campaign biography of Kennedy, written just after the inauguration, noted that

> His speeches were fact-filled, logical; his numbered arguments were well marshaled, but his speeches had little of Wilson's golden rhetoric. Often he seemed to drain the sentiment out of situations, in contrast to the first Roosevelt's showmanship and the second Roosevelt's ability to make even the mixing of cocktails in his study a dramatic performance.

Another biography of the time noted, "As a speaker he was almost professorial—serious, sincere, slightly dull."

A reporter who accompanied Kennedy in 1959 called him only a "fair speaker . . . he never waited for his audience to respond. . . . He spoke so rapidly that nothing registered." Later that same year, another reporter noted that "His stance is stiff. He is more the advocate than the orator, and lines out his speeches in a flat, hurried monotone. . . . [H]e rarely . . . builds a climax, or plucks at the heartstrings—nor, inevitably, has he often to wait for applause to die down." The same article also looked at Kennedy's likely primary opponent, Senator Hubert Humphrey. It was generally agreed that Humphrey was the superior speaker. Kennedy knew his own weakness: "I'm primarily rational rather than emotional. I need more emotion in my speeches. But at least I've got control over my subject matter and a confidence so that I can speak more and more off the cuff."

And he was determined to improve. By the time of the 1960 Wisconsin primary, he had begun to slow his delivery. A visitor to his Georgetown townhouse during the spring of 1960 found him engrossed in listening to recordings of Winston Churchill's speeches. "He kept us waiting about fifteen minutes until he heard what he wanted to hear. I guess he was listening for the cadence and style as well as the language."

He had received speech training before the campaign began, and enlisted a voice coach when strain resulted in repeated bouts of laryngitis and chronic hoarseness during the summer of 1960. The voice coach, David Blair McClosky, a professor at Boston University, worked with Kennedy on pace, relaxation, and breathing. McClosky even sat in the Senate gallery and accompanied him on early campaign trips, offering hand-signal reminders of the instructions he had offered.

Kennedy's success in the televised debates with Nixon no doubt improved his confidence. Yet an article in *Look* magazine written well after his election noted that "his oratory can be a bit breathless and grim." If Kennedy was to deliver a truly great speech at his inauguration, it would be his first.

~ He began in a hesitant tone, perhaps seeking his footing as he extemporized the salutation:

> *Vice President Johnson, Mr. Speaker, Mr. Chief Justice, President Eisenhower, Vice President Nixon, President Truman, reverend clergy, fellow citizens, we observe today not a victory of party, but a celebration of freedom—symbolizing an end, as well as a beginning— signifying renewal, as well as change.*

But now he found his voice, and it rose, as wisps of steam came from his mouth:

> *For I have sworn before you and Almighty God the same solemn oath our forebears prescribed nearly a century and three quarters ago.*

> *The world is very different now. For man holds in his mortal hands the power to abolish all forms of human poverty and all forms of human life.*

With the last phrase, for the first of many times in the course of a brief speech, Kennedy departed from his text, reducing "the power to abolish all form of human poverty and to abolish all form of human life" to a more concise expression. Similar departures, almost all apparently aimed at tightening, occurred throughout the address; changes to the text (which had already been released to reporters) were made in thirty-four places. The original reading copy appears to survive (Kennedy autographed and dated it the next morning), but it is unmarked.* It is likely that Kennedy had decided on the changes during his reading aloud that morning, or perhaps on the spur of the moment. He continued,

> *And yet the same revolutionary beliefs for which our forebears fought are still at issue around the globe—the belief that the rights of man come not from the generosity of the state, but from the hand of God.*
>
> *We dare not forget today that we are the heirs of that first revolution. Let the word go forth from this time and place, to friend and foe alike, that the torch has been passed to a new generation of Americans—born in this century, tempered by war, disciplined by a hard and bitter peace,*

It had been a "cold" and bitter peace (to play on "cold war"), but on this cold day, "hard" may have seemed a better word. Otherwise, Sorensen points out, "somebody might have laughed."

> *proud of our ancient heritage—and unwilling to witness or permit the slow undoing of those human rights to which this Nation has always been committed, and to which we are committed today at home and around the world.*

---

*Sorensen indicates that Kennedy would likely have marked such a large number of changes on his reading copy. Sorenson deputy Myer Feldman concurs. It is possible that the original reading copy was lost and that the clean version dated and autographed the next day was a duplicate.

go forth to lead the land we love,
asking His blessing and His help,
but knowing that here on earth God's
work must truly be our own.

John F. Kennedy

January 20ᵗʰ/1961

The final page of Kennedy's reading copy of the inaugural address, bearing his signature and dated January 20, 1961. Kennedy made more than thirty changes from the reading copy on delivery, and none are marked. It is possible that the original reading copy was lost, and that this clean version, autographed the next day, was a duplicate. [John F. Kennedy Library]

With the mention of a "new generation of leadership," the television cameras had panned to Eisenhower, who sat huddled in his overcoat with a scarf bundled at his throat and his top hat resting on his lap.

At this point in the speech, for the first time, Kennedy was interrupted by applause, albeit brief. But as the television cameras looked left to take in the new first lady, Jacqueline Kennedy gently closed her eyes; she was visibly transported. When she joined her husband after the speech, she touched his face and said simply, "Oh, Jack, what a day."

> *Let every nation know, whether it wishes us well or ill, that we shall pay any price, bear any burden, meet any hardship, support any friend, oppose any foe, to assure the survival and the success of liberty.*
>
> *This much we pledge—and more.*
>
> *To those old allies whose cultural and spiritual origins we share, we pledge the loyalty of faithful friends. United, there is little we cannot do in a host of cooperative ventures. Divided, there is little we can do—for we dare not meet a powerful challenge at odds and split asunder.*
>
> *To those new States whom we welcome to the ranks of the free, we pledge our word that one form of colonial control shall not have passed away merely to be replaced by a far more iron tyranny. We shall not always expect to find them supporting our view. But we shall always hope to find them strongly supporting their own freedom—and to remember that, in the past, those who foolishly sought power by riding the back of the tiger ended up inside.*

In such a serious address, this reference to a limerick was taken by some as a moment of comic relief. The applause was tinged with laughter—and at least one cry from the crowd of "Yahoo!"

To those people in the huts and villages of half the globe struggling to break the bonds of mass misery, we pledge our best effort to help them help themselves, for whatever period is required—not because the communists may be doing it, not because we seek their votes, but because it is right. If a free society cannot help the many who are poor, it cannot save the few who are rich.

This last phrase drew on a contribution by Adlai Stevenson, now slated to be Kennedy's ambassador to the United Nations. Sorensen had improved significantly on the Stevenson formulation, but even as he delivered it Kennedy refined it further, from "If *the* free society cannot help the many who are poor, it *can never* save the few who are rich" to "If *a* free society cannot help the many who are poor, it *cannot* save the few who are rich." The sentiment clearly delighted the populist Harry Truman, who smiled quickly and mischievously.

To our sister republics south of our border, we offer a special pledge— to convert our good words into good deeds—in a new alliance for progress—to assist free men and free governments in casting off the chains of poverty. But this peaceful revolution of hope cannot become the prey of hostile powers. Let all our neighbors know that we shall join with them to oppose aggression or subversion anywhere in the Americas. And let every other power know that this Hemisphere intends to remain the master of its own house.

To that world assembly of sovereign states, the United Nations, our last best hope in an age where the instruments of war have far outpaced the instruments of peace, we renew our pledge of support—to prevent it from becoming merely a forum for invective—to strengthen its shield of the new and the weak—and to enlarge the area in which its writ may run.

Finally, to those nations who would make themselves our adversary, we offer not a pledge but a request: that both sides begin anew the quest for peace, before the dark powers of destruction unleashed by science engulf all humanity in planned or accidental self-destruction.

We dare not tempt them with weakness. For only when our arms are sufficient beyond doubt can we be certain beyond doubt that they will never be employed. But neither can two great and powerful groups of nations take comfort from our present course—both sides overburdened by the cost of modern weapons, both rightly alarmed by the steady spread of the deadly atom, both racing to alter that uncertain balance of terror that stays the hand of mankind's final war.

So let us begin anew—remembering on both sides that civility is not a sign of weakness, and sincerity is always subject to proof. Let us never negotiate out of fear. But let us never fear to negotiate.

This last couplet was a Sorensen refinement of a contribution from the Harvard economist and liberal political activist John Kenneth Galbraith, now slated to be Kennedy's ambassador to India. Galbraith, characteristically, suggested it was the most memorable portion of the address.* But Kennedy actually had to pause briefly after delivering it to elicit applause. It was the only time in the speech that he would do that.

Let both sides explore what problems unite us instead of belaboring those problems which divide us.

Here Kennedy departed from his text in the first of two "which"-for-"that" substitutions. Sorensen acknowledges that confusion of these terms was his own most common grammatical error.

Let both sides, for the first time, formulate serious and precise proposals for the inspection and control of arms—and bring the

---

*Galbraith attributed the judgment to Elaine Steinbeck, and in a later recollection to John Steinbeck, but he did not dispute their conclusion.

absolute power to destroy other nations under the absolute control of all nations.

The call for arms control brought brief applause, this time unsolicited. Kennedy continued reaching out to the Soviets.

Let both sides seek to invoke the wonders of science instead of its terrors. Together let us explore the stars, conquer the deserts, eradicate disease, tap the ocean depths, and encourage the arts and commerce.

Let both sides unite to heed in all corners of the earth the command of Isaiah—to "undo the heavy burdens . . . (and) let the oppressed go free."

This was the first of only two direct quotations in the speech. Both were from the Bible, this one from the Old Testament, the later one from the New.

And if a beachhead of cooperation may push back the jungle of suspicion, let both sides join in creating a new endeavor, not a new balance of power, but a new world of law, where the strong are just and the weak secure and the peace preserved.

Here Kennedy made a substantive change. The reading copy before him envisioned the peace preserved "forever." That was more than he could bring himself to say.* He was, in his favorite summation of his own beliefs, "an idealist without illusions." With that in mind, he pressed on.

All this will not be finished in the first 100 days. Nor will it be finished in the first 1,000 days, nor in the life of this Administration, nor even perhaps in our lifetime on this planet. But let us begin.

---

*Sorensen disagrees. He sees this deletion as perhaps weakening the phrase stylistically but also as following William Strunk's admonition to "omit needless words." Sorensen says both he and Kennedy were believers in Strunk's rule. On the influence of Strunk on the Kennedy/Sorensen style, see below, pp. 86–87.

From the beginning of the address, Kennedy had confined his gestures entirely to his right hand and arm, although he used both hands to turn the pages of his speech in a loose-leaf notebook resting on the lectern. That was the essence of his style: he distrusted expansive gestures of all kinds. He once told a friend, "If I have to hold both hands above my head to be President, I'm not going to be President." Yet with "But let us begin," Kennedy reached a new level of physical intensity, tapping the podium with each word for added emphasis. The crowd reacted enthusiastically.

In your hands, my fellow citizens, more than mine, will rest the final success or failure of our course. Since this country was founded, each generation of Americans has been summoned to give testimony to its national loyalty. The graves of young Americans who answered the call to service surround the globe.

Now the trumpet summons us again—not as a call to bear arms, though arms we need; not as a call to battle, though embattled we are—but a call to bear the burden of a long twilight struggle, year in and year out, "rejoicing in hope, patient in tribulation"—a struggle against the common enemies of man: tyranny, poverty, disease, and war itself.

Can we forge against these enemies a grand and global alliance, North and South, East and West, that can assure a more fruitful life for all mankind? Will you join in that historic effort?

Just before the words "North and South," Kennedy had some difficulty turning the pages of his reading copy from page eleven to page twelve, and the confidence in his voice faltered for an instant. When he reached the end of the carryover paragraph, at first the audience seemed uncertain how to answer his question, "Will you join in that historic effort?" But "[a]fter the deep quiet the cheers came slowly. And then came distant cries of 'Yes, yes.'"

In the long history of the world, only a few generations have been
granted the role of defending freedom in its hour of maximum danger.
I do not shrink from this responsibility—I welcome it.

On the personal declaration of this last sentence, he had re-
gained his stride. His right hand was now balled in a fist, and
pounding for emphasis. The speech was reaching its emotional
climax, and the crowd seemed to sense it. This was the only
paragraph of the speech interrupted by applause. In the audience, Lincoln Kirstein reflected, "When was the last time one
thought: I would do anything this man asked me to do?"

I do not believe that any of us would exchange places with any other
people or any other generation. The energy, the faith, the devotion
which we bring to this endeavor will light our country and all who
serve it—and the glow from that fire can truly light the world.

Kennedy was nearly shouting now,

And so, my fellow Americans: ask not what your country can do for
you—ask what you can do for your country.

If this was, in effect, another question, the crescendo of applause provided an immediate answer.

My fellow citizens of the world: ask not what America will do for
you, but what together we can do for the freedom of man.

Even though this second formulation was something of an
anticlimax, the crowd was his now, and applauded again, even as
Kennedy softened his tone, moving to conclude on a prayerful
note.

Finally, whether you are citizens of America or citizens of the world,
ask of us here the same high standards of strength and sacrifice which
we ask of you. With a good conscience our only sure reward, with

history the final judge of our deeds, let us go forth to lead the land we love, asking His blessing and His help, but knowing that here on earth God's work must truly be our own.

The work of the speech was done. Kennedy clasped both his hands in those of Johnson before turning to Eisenhower. Nixon somewhat desperately reached across the platform's aisle to touch the new president again, and they shook hands one more time as the crowd cheered long and loudly.

The address had comprised 1,345 words and had taken less than 14 minutes to deliver. It was the most important speech Kennedy had ever given—and it had been only about two weeks since he had first seen a working draft.

Part Two

The Making of the Inaugural Address, 1961

I
———

When

The greatest inaugural address in American history is al-most certainly Lincoln's second. The conclusion of that speech ranks with the most enduring words ever spoken in the United States; the full speech is literally chiseled in stone in the Memorial to Lincoln in Washington. Speaking after nearly four years of Civil War (and just five weeks before war's end), Lincoln ended his address this way:

> Fondly do we hope, fervently do we pray, that this mighty scourge of war may speedily pass away. Yet, if God wills that it continue until all the wealth piled by the bondsman's two hundred and fifty years of unrequited toil shall be sunk, and until every drop of blood drawn with the lash shall be paid by another drawn with the sword, as was said three thousand years ago, so still it must be said "the judgments of the Lord are true and righteous altogether."
>
> With malice toward none, with charity for all, with firmness in the right as God gives us to see the right, let us strive on to finish the work we are in, to bind up the nation's wounds, to care for him who shall have borne the battle and

for his widow and his orphan, to do all which may achieve and cherish a just and lasting peace among ourselves and with all nations.

This is the standard by which John Kennedy knew any inaugural address aspiring to greatness would be judged. In early preparation for his own speech, he asked Ted Sorensen to read all previous inaugurals and to give particular attention to Lincoln's rhetoric in his even better-known Gettysburg Address. Sorensen did so, noting that "Lincoln never used a two- or three-syllable word where a one-syllable word would do, and never used two or three words where one word would do."

Word count thus became a fixation in the preparation of Kennedy's speech. Sorensen or an assistant estimated the number of words in Woodrow Wilson's addresses from 1913 and 1917, FDR's from 1941, and the most recent address, Eisenhower's in 1957.* The average inaugural address had run 2,500 words. Kennedy directed, according to a note taken by Sorensen, that they "make it shortest since T.R. [Theodore Roosevelt's 987 words in 1905] (except for FDR's abbreviated war-time remarks [554 words] in 1945)." Not counting Kennedy's longer salutation than the one FDR used in 1941, this goal was achieved.

What is perhaps most remarkable about Lincoln's second inaugural, however, is not its brevity at 703 words (the Gettysburg Address was just 272 words) but the fact noted by Ronald White, whose book about it is called *Lincoln's Greatest Speech*: "We have

---

*Given the inaccuracy of Sorensen's counts, it can be assumed that all were estimates, perhaps based on line counts in a printed version. The estimates (and actual counts) are as follows: Wilson, 1913, 1,690 words (1,709); Wilson, 1917, 1,485 words (1,545); Roosevelt, 1941, 1,281 words (1,344); Eisenhower, 1957, 1,730 words (1,678).

United States Senate

MEMORANDUM

Roosevelt	1941	1281 words
Wilson	1917	1485 words
Wilson	1913	1690 words
Eisenhower	1957	1730 words
TCS draft		1693 words

-413

1280

Shorter than   Eisenhower 2   FDR's 1st & 2nd
                 Hoover
                 Coolidge
                 Harding
                 Taft
                 McKinley
                 Wilson's 2

Undated typewritten/handwritten notes from Sorensen's file on the length of previous inaugural addresses. Note the reference to a "TCS draft" of 1693 words. Just below this, in pencil, Sorensen subtracted 413 from 1693 to yield the figure 1280. This is probably the approximate word-count of the draft Sorensen gave to Kennedy, which appears (minus its missing first page) as Appendix B. Sorensen's handwritten notes on the bottom half of the sheet say:

Shorter than   Eisenhower 2   FDR's 1st & 2nd
                 Hoover
                 Coolidge
                 Harding
                 Taft
                 McKinley
                 Wilson's 2

[John F. Kennedy Library]

no evidence of any editorial counsel in the preparation of the Second Inaugural Address."*

That was not a model John Kennedy wished to follow.

From the outset, Kennedy expected his inaugural address to draw on the talents of many of those around him, and especially on Sorensen's rhetorical gifts. But discretion was also a paramount concern. Sorensen's notes of the same early conversation with Kennedy say "leave no copies around, even RNG-MF." That is, Kennedy did not want Sorensen showing copies of his work on the inaugural even to his own closest associates, Richard Goodwin, who had recently joined Kennedy's Senate staff as a writer, and Myer Feldman, the campaign research chief.

᧥ On the evening of Thursday, November 24, 1960, John and Jacqueline Kennedy had Thanksgiving dinner at home in Georgetown, enjoying caviar and champagne with their friend Bill Walton. After dinner, around eight o'clock, the president-elect left for Palm Beach aboard his own airplane; Mrs. Kennedy, more than eight months pregnant, remained behind. While her husband was airborne, however, Jacqueline Kennedy went into labor, called her doctor, and was soon taken to Georgetown University Hospital. John Kennedy was notified of the labor over the airplane's radio just before his arrival in Florida. Once on the ground, he ordered the faster press plane refueled and comman-

---

*Note that this was not the case with Lincoln's first inaugural address, for which the peroration was molded by Lincoln from a suggestion by his incoming secretary of state, William Seward; Lincoln also received editorial assistance on his first inaugural from his friends O. H. Browning and Judge David Davis, and from elder statesman Francis Blair, Sr. Assistance in writing inaugural addresses has a rich tradition. George Washington's first inaugural, for instance, was based in significant measure on a draft by James Madison.

deered it for a quick return to Washington. He learned of the birth of his son and namesake shortly before takeoff and arrived at the hospital at 4:18 A.M.

Ted Sorensen also had a productive night. His Thanksgiving dinner took place in the home of Myer Feldman. After dinner, Sorensen retired to a basement den and wrote what Feldman, who later worked some in motion pictures, calls a "treatment" for the inaugural address. It consisted of a "stream of thoughts" or "chain of thoughts," "a sketch." It was "more than notes" and "more than an outline" but was "not a finished speech." Sorensen vaguely recalls that he did some "early work" on the inaugural at Feldman's home that evening, but has no specific recollection of what it involved.

But Sorensen's Thanksgiving evening work, contrary to the account in a recent book, was in no sense the "first draft" of the speech. Feldman, who did not see the "treatment" the night it was written but did review it on an airplane flight with Sorensen in December, confirms that it is his impression that drafting by Sorensen did not begin until many weeks later, and that Kennedy "probably did not" ever see the "treatment." "There would have been no reason for him to have" seen it. Moreover, Sorensen respected Kennedy's wish that he not show drafts to Feldman; Feldman saw a draft of the speech itself close to the time of delivery, and then only when Kennedy showed it to him. Sorensen confirms that he did not show drafts to Feldman and states repeatedly that drafting did not begin until much later.

ᔜ But Sorensen was not the only person who was committing to paper thoughts about what Kennedy should say in his inaugural address. John Kenneth Galbraith was another. In late 1960, Glabraith was fifty-two years old, a professor of economics at

Harvard, and a leader of liberal Democrats. For his first twenty-three years he had lived and studied agricultural economics in rural Ontario, Canada; he had become a U.S. citizen in his late twenties. In the late 1930s Galbraith taught at Harvard (where Joseph Kennedy, Jr., was among his students) and then at Princeton before becoming a self-described wartime "price fixer" at the Office of Price Administration and later a member of the Strategic Bombing Survey team. He returned to Harvard in 1949 and the next year published *American Capitalism: The Concept of Countervailing Power*, then, in 1958, *The Affluent Society*. The former book called for repeated government intervention in the economy to quell inflation; the latter condemned excess consumerism.

Galbraith was brilliant: witty, urbane, a gifted speaker and writer, and lent his talents to Adlai Stevenson's 1952 and 1956 presidential campaigns. But, like Stevenson, he was an elitist who seemed at once to revel in politics and to find it somehow beneath him.

On the afternoon of December 23, 1960, Galbraith came to Kennedy's father's home in Palm Beach, where Kennedy spent much of the transition, to confer with the president-elect on a range of subjects, including an important discussion on farm policy, on which Galbraith was an expert. Kennedy had asked Galbraith on December 7 to serve as U.S. ambassador to India. Galbraith had been more interested in assuming Kennedy's U.S. Senate seat from Massachusetts but had accepted the India posting. (Kennedy later called India Galbraith's "period of penance." Galbraith wrote in his memoirs: "Kennedy, I've always believed, was pleased to have me in his administration but at a suitable distance such as in India.")

On arrival in Palm Beach, Galbraith presented Kennedy with a complete draft of an inaugural address. It ran to thirteen triple-spaced typed pages. There is no indication that Kennedy solicited the draft; Sorensen says that, "knowing Ken, it wouldn't have taken a solicitation." Galbraith himself had noted in a letter to Kennedy shortly after the election: "Along with people who like to hear themselves talk, there are, unquestionably, some who are even more inordinately attracted by their own composition. I may well be entitled to gold star membership in both groups."

Galbraith more recently recalled that he and Kennedy "were working in close association and [the draft] might well have been a suggestion of the moment." With respect to whether the draft was solicited or not, Galbraith says, "On some matters of history there is neither record nor knowledge. Fortunately, as here, it may not be vital."

Kennedy and Galbraith spent a good bit of time conferring that afternoon. The inaugural address was one of the subjects they discussed. Evelyn Lincoln, in a memo written twenty-six years later, says they talked about the "tone and tenor" of the speech. A letter from Galbraith to Kennedy just seventeen days after the event refers to "changes [Kennedy] suggested" in the draft.

Galbraith was clearly angling for a central role in the creation of the inaugural address. The previous July, on the morning after Kennedy had delivered his acceptance speech at the Democratic National Convention in Los Angeles, Galbraith had sent the new nominee an extraordinary letter.

Kennedy's speech had declared that "It is time, in short, for a new generation of leadership." And it marked the debut of the term New Frontier. "[T]he New Frontier of which I speak," Kennedy had said, "is not a set of promises—it is a set of challenges. It sums up not what I intend to offer the American people, but what I intend to ask of them."

But Galbraith was unimpressed. He had been a Kennedy floor manager at the convention but had returned home to Cambridge,

Massachusetts, before the speech. Listening to it on television, Galbraith saw deficiencies all around:

> In the first place, your speech last night was essentially unfinished. It was badly in need of editing and polish. As a purely literary matter, the sentences could have been greatly smoothed. The images could have been much sharper and more vivid. Some superfluous words could have been drained out. The transitions could have been far smoother and more skillful. Your small transitions and changes of pace were insufficiently marked off from your major ones.

Calling this a "problem of editing," Galbraith hastened to write, "I hope that this won't be taken as criticism of anyone who worked on the speech. I am aware of the pressure."

But the criticism came at a sensitive moment, as Sorensen had been "pushed a little into the background" and, for the moment, "wasn't quite so close to Kennedy as he had been" in the years before the primary campaign.

Nor were the writers and editors the only ones Galbraith saw at fault. The candidate himself, the professor noted, was a master of "straightforward exposition and argument." But,

> When it comes to oratorical flights and Stevenson-type rhetoric, you give a reasonable imitation of a bird with a broken wing. You do get off the ground but it's wearing on the audience to keep wondering if you are going to stay up.
>
> The solution here is simple. You cannot avoid these flights into space entirely—they are part of our political ritual. And maybe you could be less self-consciously awful in their performance although personally I would be sorry if you were. But the real answer is to keep this part of the speechmaking to the absolute minimum.

Galbraith's attitude toward Kennedy was not unusual among Stevensonian liberals. Arthur Schlesinger, writing during the fall campaign in *defense* of Kennedy, was nevertheless breathtakingly condescending:

> The character of Kennedy's mind is worth considering. If it is less scholarly than Wilson's, less bold and adventurous than Franklin Roosevelt's, less rich and reflective than Adlai Stevenson's, it has nonetheless qualities of its own.

If Kennedy was offended by this attitude, there is no record of it. He had mangled the timing of his convention acceptance peroration in Los Angeles, and had been hampered by the needs in the speech to enlist each of his primary opponents by name and to attack Nixon directly and personally. Some of the speech had simply flown over the heads of much of the audience, with historical allusions to David Lloyd George's warning against a "Tory nation" and to Presidents Pierce, Buchanan, McKinley, Taft, and Harding.

What's more, Kennedy had delivered the address in an outdoor arena, facing into a setting sun, and had had difficulty reading his text. His disappointment in his own performance in the acceptance speech had, as noted, provoked his resolve to take extra steroids on such occasions in the future.

But the second half of the acceptance speech had been much stronger than the first, and the text had been generally well received. When asked about the Galbraith letter many years later—long after the general election campaign had restored his relationship with Kennedy—Sorensen's first reaction was to note of the six-foot-eight-inch Galbraith that "Ken is a towering figure in many ways." Sorensen then drew the obvious conclusion: "I think that letter clearly says, from then on 'you should have

[Galbraith] as your speech editor, if not your speech writer.'"
Galbraith became neither.

Galbraith says:

> I never suggested that I replace Ted Sorensen. I may have
> offered some assistance, indicated that I was eager to help, but
> I always assumed that Ted was there for the duration, a major
> figure, as he had been in the campaign and before. I cannot
> think that anyone with any sense of reality and purpose could
> have thought of replacing him. Any such interpretation of my
> letter to Kennedy is surely wrong.

Kennedy did continue to welcome Galbraith's advice, and
the Galbraith draft inaugural does seem to have spurred action.
Until this point, forty-five days into the transition period,
Kennedy had been focused on personnel selection and policy reviews. He had begun announcing cabinet choices on December
1 and completed them on December 17. Sorensen's energies had
been devoted largely to a series of task forces on various policy
matters. A full-day session to review the task-force reports had
been held in Palm Beach on December 21. After one or two initial conversations, and now with just four weeks to go before the
inauguration, little work had been done on the inaugural address
beyond the Thanksgiving "treatment."

To some extent this was almost certainly by design. The
scholar Richard Neustadt's transition advice to Kennedy had
included the following paragraph on "preparing the inaugural
address":

> It would be well not to begin this too early, but instead to
> wait until the first lines of a message—that is to say of an
> initial program—had emerged. The inaugural address has
> to be a tone-setter. It will help to have a notion of what is

to follow before spending much time on this introduction. It will also help to wait until one knows what international and economic conditions to expect by January 20.

Franklin Roosevelt, for example, had first read Raymond Moley's proposed draft of the 1933 inaugural address just five days before delivering the speech.

On the same day Kennedy met in Palm Beach with Galbraith, he asked Sorensen to solicit help with the speech. Sorensen now speculates that, "maybe after getting Galbraith's draft, JFK called me and said, 'Better get cracking.'" Sorensen did so by sending a "block wire" telegram:

> The President-Elect has asked me to collect any suggestions you may have for the Inaugural Address. In view of the short period of time available before Inauguration Day, it would be appreciated if we could have your recommendations by December 31. We are particularly interested in specific themes and in language to articulate these themes whether it takes one page or ten pages. Many many thanks.
>
> Theodore C. Sorensen
Special Counsel to the
President-Elect

Copies of the wire went to ten men, most of them slated to join the Kennedy administration. Rockefeller Foundation president and former diplomat Dean Rusk had been nominated as secretary of state; former Connecticut governor Chester Bowles would be Rusk's deputy secretary. Douglas Dillon, Bowles's predecessor as deputy secretary in the Eisenhower administration, would be Kennedy's secretary of the treasury. The labor lawyer Arthur Goldberg would be labor secretary. The California political veteran Fred Dutton would serve as a White House assistant. From outside the government, the writer Joseph Kraft had helped Sorensen from time to time and would continue to do so. David Lloyd was executive director of Americans for Democratic Action, a leading liberal group. Allan Nevins, who had contributed a draft of the convention acceptance speech with the concept of a "new frontier" (although not the actual phrase), was a leading American historian who had written the foreword to *Profiles in Courage* and had lent his imprimatur as nominal editor of a book of Kennedy's foreign policy speeches selected for publication by Sorensen and the attorney Harris Wofford.* Kennedy had, just two weeks earlier, written to the editor Evan Thomas: "I enjoy Nevins' reflections on historical events more than any other writer I know."

Presumably to obscure Kennedy's tracks from Sorensen's view, a copy of the wire was also directed to be sent to Professor John Kenneth Galbraith in Cambridge.

The other person to whom a request for a draft was sent was Adlai Stevenson, Kennedy's principal rival within the Democratic party, and generally in 1960 regarded as the most eloquent man in American politics. Stevenson had been born to political privilege, the son of Grover Cleveland's second-term vice president. The younger Stevenson had practiced law in Chicago and

---

*Nevins' draft of the acceptance speech begins with the symbolism of the convention meeting in the West, on the old frontier. But the closest Nevins came to the later-famous phrase was the line, "We must search for frontiers that are not geographic." Arthur Schlesinger gave a speech in March 1960 entitled "New Frontiers of American Liberalism," but it was Sorensen who adopted the phrase "new frontier" as the leitmotif of the acceptance speech. For that speech Kennedy and Sorensen had solicited drafts not only from Nevins but also from James MacGregor Burns, Henry Steele Commager, John Fischer of *Harper's*, Max Freedman of the *Washington Post*, Mark De-Wolfe Howe, Sidney Hyman, Earl Latham of Amherst, Walt Rostow, Arthur Schlesinger, and Gore Vidal. Of these ten men, only Nevins was also asked for a draft of the inaugural address, though Rostow and Schlesinger worked with Galbraith on his drafts and Vidal volunteered language unbidden.

WESTERN UNION
TELEGRAM
W. P. MARSHALL, PRESIDENT

DOMESTIC SERVICE
Check the class of service desired; otherwise this message will be sent as a fast telegram
TELEGRAM
DAY LETTER
NIGHT LETTER

INTERNATIONAL SERVICE
Check the class of service desired, otherwise the message will be sent at the full rate
FULL RATE
LETTER TELEGRAM
SHORE SHIP

NO. WDS.-CL. OF SVC. | PD. OR COLL. | CASH NO. | CHARGE TO THE ACCOUNT OF | TIME FILED

SENATOR KENNEDY - OFFICIAL | DEC. 23, 1960

Send the following message, subject to the terms on back hereof, which are hereby agreed to

BLOCK WIRE

Dr. Allan Nevins
Huntington Library and Art Gallery
1151 Oxford Road
San Marino 9, California

Hon. Adlai E. Stevenson
135 South LaSalle Street
Chicago 3, Illinois

Mr. Douglas Dillon
Hobe Sound
Florida

Mr. Joseph Kraft
1148 Fifth Avenue
New York, New York

Hon. Chester Bowles
Hayden's Point
Essex, Connecticut

Mr. Arthur Goldberg
1001 Connecticut Avenue, N.W.
Washington, D. C.

Mr. Dean Rusk
21 Fenimore Road
Scarsdale, New York

Mr. Fred Dutton
1131 11th Avenue
Sacramento, California

Mr. David Lloyd
1329 18th Street, N.W.
Washington, D. C.

Prof. J. K. Galbraith
30 Francis Avenue
Cambridge, Massachusetts

The President-Elect has asked me to collect any suggestions you may have for the Inaugural Address. In view of the short period of time available before Inauguration Day, it would be appreciated if we could have your recommendations by December 31. We are particularly interested in specific themes and in language to articulate these themes whether it takes one page or ten pages. Many many thanks.

Theodore C. Sorensen
Special Counsel to the
President-Elect

Block wire dated December 23, 1960, from Sorensen on Kennedy's behalf, soliciting inaugural drafts from ten men. Earlier on the day this wire was sent, Kennedy met with Galbraith and received his inaugural draft. Sorensen now speculates, "Maybe after getting Galbraith's draft, JFK called me and said, 'Better get cracking.'" [John F. Kennedy Library] worked in Washington for the Agricultural Adjustment Administration, the Alcohol Control Administration, and the Departments of Navy and State. In 1948 he was elected governor of Illinois and had championed reform in Springfield. Drafted for president with Truman's support in 1952, he had pursued the prize again in 1956 and, belatedly (and to Kennedy's great annoyance), in 1960. Kennedy had designated him as ambassador to the United Nations in the new administration, refusing Stevenson the post he had sought—secretary of state.

The Kennedys considered Stevenson weak and somehow a bit effeminate, though the divorced Stevenson's appeal to women was well known. Stevenson's ambivalent and sometimes haughty attitude toward politics seemed summed up in the perhaps apocryphal story of a voter telling him that "every thinking American" would vote for him for president, only to be met with the candidate's retort, "Yes, but I need a majority." But Stevenson's facility with words was unquestioned.

Stevenson responded to Kennedy and Sorensen's call with what he called "some hurried paragraphs," actually ten pages of such paragraphs, followed by an eight-page disquisition, though he complained about the time pressure. He confined himself to foreign policy, with just a few passing mentions of the civil rights issue at home. Bowles submitted a draft on behalf of himself and Rusk that has also been preserved. Dillon offered an outline and some written notes. Nevins and Kraft both prepared and submitted drafts, but both have apparently been lost. There is no indication of any response by Goldberg, Dutton, or Lloyd, and Sorensen recalls none. Galbraith worked up a second draft of his proposal, on which he, in turn, solicited and received assistance from Arthur Schlesinger and Walt Rostow. Unsolicited advice and drafts came from others, but, in all, Kennedy and Sorensen had before them at least five *solicited* draft speeches when they began work on the inaugural address.

First, however, there was another major speech to be written and delivered.

On January 9, Kennedy went to Cambridge and Boston to attend a meeting of the Harvard Overseers, meet designated and prospective staffers at Schlesinger's home, and deliver a farewell address to the Massachusetts Legislature. Kennedy drew the idea for such a speech from Lincoln's farewell to the people of Springfield a hundred years earlier. But this set the rhetorical bar very high, and Sorensen "had reluctantly dipped into the file of phrases collected for the Inaugural Address" to meet this standard. Kennedy was concerned they "were using up some of our best lines for the inaugural."

Sorensen does not now recall what phrases or lines he borrowed, though he confirms that no inaugural draft had yet been written at this point. The highlights of the Boston address were a quotation from the Pilgrim leader John Winthrop "that we shall be as a city upon a hill—the eyes of all people are upon us." And then Kennedy set himself and his listeners tests for their future conduct of office:

> First, were we truly men of courage—with the courage to stand up to one's enemies—and the courage to stand up, when necessary, to one's own associates—the courage to resist public pressure as well as private greed?
>
> Secondly, were we men of judgment—with perceptive judgment of the future as well as the past—of our own mistakes as well as the mistakes of others—with enough wisdom to know what we did not know, and enough candor to admit it?

Third, were we truly men of integrity—men who never ran out on either the principles in which we believed or the people who believed in us—men whom neither financial gain nor political ambition could ever divert from the fulfillment of our sacred trust?

Finally, were we truly men of dedication—with an honor mortgaged to no single individual or group, and compromised by no private obligation or aim, but devoted solely to serving the public good and the national interest?

These words echoed Franklin Roosevelt's 1932 tribute to the Sorensen family hero, Senator George Norris—a tribute quoted in *Profiles in Courage*:

History asks, "Did the man have integrity?"
"Did the man have unselfishness?"
"Did the man have courage?"
"Did the man have consistency?"

It was a demanding standard—both for service and as rhetoric. Kennedy worried, over the next ten days, "that it would be hard to top."

ᔈ Shortly after completing work on the Boston speech—but likely some days before its delivery—Sorensen sat down to write a first draft of the inaugural address by hand, probably on a legal pad. (He always composed in longhand.) Little survives of that draft. Sorensen quoted four sentences from it in his 1965 book *Kennedy*, trimming two of them slightly as he edited the book; the original, longer versions, from Sorensen's handwritten manuscript for *Kennedy*, are reproduced in Appendix A. All three sentences in the first draft that correspond to passages in the earliest surviving draft were changed between those two drafts.

When asked what became of the first draft quoted in *Kennedy*, Sorensen says it does not now exist. When asked how he came to quote from it in his book, he states that he had it with him at the time he wrote the book in 1964–1965. Finally, when asked if he destroyed the first draft of the Kennedy inaugural address, Sorensen declines to comment. Noting that some have claimed, over the years, to have the first draft of the speech, he rejoins, "I know they don't."

This is a very sensitive point, and especially so for Sorensen himself. He resolutely maintains that he was not the principal author of the speech. At once wistful and determined, he says, "I recognize that I have some obligation to history, but all these years I have tried to make clear that President Kennedy was the principal author of all his speeches and articles. If I say otherwise, that diminishes him, and I don't want to diminish him."

Asked what would be so terrible about the revelation that a busy executive, compelled to form a national government, develop a budget, and establish a complete range of public policies in just ten weeks, had turned to an accomplished, familiar, and trusted collaborator to craft a speech, Sorensen observes, "The speech was a special speech. Some people think its words are holy, and the more so because they come from JFK. So I'm not going to change that."

But there is more to it than that. There is *Profiles in Courage*. The book was published in 1956 and the next year awarded the Pulitzer Prize for biography. Sorensen's assistance was acknowledged in the book, but John F. Kennedy was listed as the sole author. Others thought, and said, nearly from the outset that this was a misrepresentation.

Asked if part of his concern about establishing Kennedy's authorship of the inaugural address is tied to the 1957 controversy stirred up by columnist Drew Pearson's allegation on Mike

Wallace's ABC television broadcast, and later more specifically in print, that Sorensen, not Kennedy, wrote *Profiles in Courage*, Sorensen says, "Of course." Pearson and ABC later retracted the allegation under significant pressure from Kennedy and in the face of denials by Sorensen—and, it should be noted, in an era before the case of *New York Times Co. v. Sullivan* revolutionized the American law of libel in favor of defendants. The controversy remained live, however. At the first meeting between Kennedy and Robert McNamara, in December 1960—to discuss the possibility of McNamara joining the Kennedy cabinet—McNamara pointedly asked Kennedy if he had really written *Profiles in Courage*. Kennedy said he had, and told others he admired McNamara's forthrightness in asking. More recently, McNamara has said he "came away with the firm conclusion that the book represented Kennedy's thinking, even if many of the words were written by Ted." But Sorensen says that Kennedy "felt very strongly" about *Profiles in Courage*, was extremely proud of the Pulitzer Prize he had been awarded for writing it, and that Pearson's and other similar, whispered charges "upset him a great deal." Pressed to compare the writing process for *Profiles in Courage* and the inaugural address, Sorensen says "the underlying realities are similar." He also says that the carefully crafted sentence of acknowledgment to him in the preface to *Profiles in Courage* is "quite an accurate statement." The sentence is: "The greatest debt is owed to my research associate, Theodore C. Sorensen, for his invaluable assistance in the assembly and preparation of the material upon which this book is based."

Whether the sentence, while not inaccurate, understates Sorensen's role is beyond the scope of this book. But we know that Kennedy had planned for Sorensen to ghostwrite another book—on New England's economic problems—on his behalf just months before work began on *Profiles in Courage*. And Herbert Parmet, a Kennedy biographer who examined the relevant files, concluded that Kennedy "served principally as an overseer or, more charitably, as a sponsor or editor" of *Profiles in Courage.* "[T]he burdens of time and literary craftsmanship were clearly Sorensen's, and he gave the book both the drama and the flow that made for its readability."

∾ The historical record with respect to the inaugural address is clear, or now should be. Sorensen wrote in *Kennedy*, and now confirms in interviews, that no draft of the speech was begun until after the drafting of Kennedy's address to the Massachusetts Legislature had been completed. So the first draft was written no earlier than shortly before January 9, the date of the Boston speech.

The undated memorandum on U.S. Senate letterhead in Sorensen's inaugural address file, reflecting his attempt to count words in the addresses of Wilson, FDR, and Eisenhower, also contains a word count—of 1,693 words—for a "TCS draft." In pencil just below this typescript, the number 413 is subtracted, and a sum found, 1,280. This confirms the point: a Theodore C. Sorensen draft of 1,693 words was edited down to 1,280 words. The longer version was presumably Sorensen's first draft.

Some notes scribbled by Sorensen suggest that he may have done this word counting and editing at Kennedy's instance, after Kennedy saw the first draft. The same sheet that contains Kennedy's injunction to "count words" in "Ike '57, FDR '41, Wilson, '17, Wilson, '13," and to "make it shortest since T.R. (except for FDR's abbreviated wartime ceremony in 1945)," also remind Sorensen to "count words in draft" and to "shorten sentences & words" and "add style & eloquence."

The earliest surviving draft of the inaugural address is found not in Sorensen's files, however, but in President Kennedy's. It is a five-page typewritten document, with the pages numbered two through six; that is, the first page of a six-page draft is missing. The draft is reproduced in Appendix B. Its structure quite closely corresponds to that of the final speech, and the missing first page would seem to have included material corresponding to the first two paragraphs of the final version. Not counting the concluding paragraph, which was added to the draft in Sorensen's handwriting, it comes to 1,295 words. If we allow for the same sort of error found in Sorensen's word counting of earlier inaugural addresses, this earliest surviving draft would seem to be the edited version of the Sorensen draft, or at least something very close to it. This shortened version will be referred to as the "TCS Draft."

It is found in Kennedy's file, presumably, because Sorensen gave it to Kennedy in Boston on or about January 9, or sent it to the president-elect in Florida for review shortly before that. Sorensen is confident that the draft in Kennedy's file represents Sorensen's "working draft" from sometime during the period before he traveled from Washington to Palm Beach on the evening of Sunday, January 15, to work in person with Kennedy on the speech.

But the TCS Draft was by no means the work of Sorensen alone. It reflected general direction from Kennedy and drew many passages from Kennedy campaign speeches. The president-elect told Sorensen:

> He wanted it focused on foreign policy. He did not want it to sound partisan, pessimistic or critical of his predecessor. He wanted neither the customary cold war rhetoric about the Communist menace nor any weasel words that Khrushchev might misinterpret. And he wanted it to set a tone for the era about to begin.

Moreover, Sorensen had before him, in preparing this document, drafts from at least five other men: Stevenson, Galbraith,

In your hands, my fellow citizens, more than mine, lie the final answer. Were we to suffer open armed attack, our decision would be clear, our response instant, our dedication to the cause complete. We would not pause to count the cost or weigh the odds. We would not heed the voices of surrender, fear or panic. Every man and every woman would answer to the call of the trumpet.

Today the trumpet sounds its urgent call again -- not a call to arms, though arms we need -- not a call to battle though embattled we are -- but a call to a broader, more basic struggle against all the enemies of man -- tyranny and poverty and war itself.

Will you join heart and soul in that historic battle? Will you give to the defense of self-government the same full measure of self-denial you would give to the fight for self-survival?

If we fail now, we fail our heirs, our forbears and all mankind. But if we prevail -- if at the end of the tunnel of darkness we find the light -- then shall we fulfill the dreams of those who love this land most not for what it was, not for what it is, but for what it can and will someday be.

So ask not what your country is going to do for you. Ask what you can do for your country. Ask of your leaders the same high standards and sacrifice that we will ask of you. And ask the Lord above to grant us all the strength and wisdom we shall need. WITH A CLEAR CONSCIENCE OUR ONLY SURE REWARD, WITH HISTORY THE FINAL JUDGE OF OUR MOTIVES, LET US GO FORTH TO LEAD THE LAND WE LOVE, ASKING HIS blessing AND HELP, BUT KNOWING THAT HERE ON EARTH GOD'S WORK MUST TRULY BE OUR OWN.

The last page of the "TCS draft," found in Kennedy's files. This is the earliest surviving draft of the speech. The peroration added at the bottom is in Sorensen's handwriting. [John F. Kennedy Library]

Allan Nevins, Joseph Kraft, and Chester Bowles. A memorandum of suggestions and an accompanying draft from the pollster Lou Harris came to Kennedy on or about January 14. Although the Nevins and Kraft drafts appear to be lost, there is reason to believe that some of their language made it into the TCS Draft.*

That is not the case for the Harris draft or the Bowles draft, submitted on behalf of both Bowles and Rusk. The Bowles/Rusk draft, headed a "Suggested Outline For Inaugural Message," consists of eleven numbered points on twelve typewritten pages. The language is largely unremarkable. ("No administration at any previous watershed in American history started with all the answers to the dangers and complicated problems confronting it. But each of them understood the simple truth that answers had to be found.") Sorensen used none of it, perhaps in part because of some distaste for Bowles personally. Sorensen, for instance, later recalled his meeting with Bowles in 1960 to obtain his endorsement for the Kennedy campaign: "He told me of his own potential following for the Presidency, his chances for the Cabinet under other candidates, his unwillingness to campaign against Humphrey, and his hope

---

*A letter from Nevins to Sorensen in Sorensen's files, dated December 29, 1960, says, "Here is a suggestion of one particular tone and set of ideas that seems to me practicable. I have given it so much work that I hope you will read it carefully." Unfortunately, the enclosure is not in the file nor elsewhere in the Kennedy Library or in Nevins's papers at Columbia University. Kennedy Library staff confirms that Thurston Clarke errs when he says that the Nevins draft is in Sorensen's files, and thus presumably also errs in stating as a fact that none of the Nevins draft was used. Sorensen recalls a submission from Kraft, and Kraft recalled that "I did do a draft of the Inaugural at Ted's request, some of which got used but all of which got transformed." Sorensen recalls that Kraft "was a very close friend, he wrote very well, he understood Kennedy and understood me, and I would have paid attention to his draft." But the Kraft draft cannot be found at the Kennedy Library nor in Kraft's papers, which are also located at Columbia University. Efforts to locate the Nevins and Kraft drafts through their families were also unsuccessful.

that Kennedy, if unable to win a convention majority, might throw all his support behind him."

Rusk, too, was already on the way to being marginalized within the administration—he had, for instance, accepted the job of secretary of state after Kennedy had already named four men who would be Rusk's principal subordinates (Bowles, Stevenson, Averill Harriman, and G. Mennen Williams), each of them a former governor of a state.

Galbraith and Stevenson were another matter. Both were highly talented writers. The TCS Draft contains three passages drawn from Galbraith—including the later-famous phrases "a thousand days" and "never fear to negotiate"—and eight taken from Stevenson. Galbraith later wrote, "A ghost writer is like an unloved dog in a poor family. He must be content with scraps. The Kennedy-Sorensen draft, though less daring, was probably a lot wiser than mine."

For all his skill with words, however, Galbraith missed a key point about a presidential speech in the new age of television. He gave Kennedy his second draft, fifteen triple-spaced pages, in Cambridge on January 9 and accompanied it with a letter volunteering to produce a final draft as well. But he also wrote,

> This is preeminently a speech for those who will read it rather than those who will hear it. The immediate audience will not long remember. The readers will render the ultimate decision. So, rightly, I believe, I have made few concessions to your speaking style.

In fact, as Galbraith later acknowledged—and as he knew Kennedy agreed—Galbraith's own style was derivative of Adlai Stevenson's. Galbraith also declined to include a peroration in his draft, telling Kennedy, "I suppose [it] must evoke God on some rising note . . . [but] no man can write another's prayers."

Nor did Galbraith exaggerate when he said he had made few concessions to Kennedy's style. While the Galbraith draft began by promising to speak "plainly and without pretense of rhetoric" and later pledged a "new era of plain speaking," it also used words such as "surcease" and "penuriousness," made references to the three-toed sloth, and said that "all seek to avoid the Walpurgis Night." Galbraith's cover letter called these "attention pieces." But they must have grated on both Kennedy and Sorensen. Sorensen later listed some of their key guidelines for Kennedy speeches:

- "The test of a text was not how it appeared to the eye but how it sounded to the ear."
- "He used little or no slang, dialect, legalistic terms, contractions, clichés, elaborate metaphors or ornate figures of speech."
- "The intellectual level of his speeches showed erudition but not arrogance."

Years later Galbraith acknowledged that "I never could capture [Kennedy's] meter. He talked in short, choppy sentences. I am more orotund."

Sorensen did make use of Galbraith's drafts, and especially of Stevenson's,* but he honed the language in each case, paring, sharpening, and improving it, adding force. A side-by-side comparison is instructive:

---

*Interestingly, one phrase, because "it is right," appears in both the Stevenson and Galbraith drafts. Harris Wofford speculates that both may have gotten the phrase from Chester Bowles, but the phrase is used somewhat differently in the two drafts and does not appear in the draft Bowles himself submitted. Galbraith and Stevenson did not confer directly on the speech, though Galbraith did aid Stevenson in preparing the latter's 1960 speeches; perhaps it is just a coincidence.

STEVENSON	SORENSEN
We have not seen one form of colonial control superceded simply to see another far more iron and more implacable system take its place.	we pledge our word that one form of colonial control shall not have passed merely to be replaced by a far more iron tyranny.
We cannot expect them to be actively on our side. Why should they be? We do want them to be vigilantly and intelligently on the side of their own freedom and integrity.	we shall not always expect to find you on our side. But we shall always expect to find you vigorously on the side of your freedom . . .
We will do this not because of anything the Russians may say or do, but because it is right . . .	not because our enemies are doing it, not because we seek your votes, but because it is right.
We cannot allow our instruments of war to outpace the instruments of peace and construction.	The instruments of war have far outpaced the instruments of peace.
we dare not tempt them with weakness.	We dare not tempt you with weakness.
united for common purposes there is little we cannot do to advance peace and well-being; disunited, there is little we can do. . . . we cannot deal with the Communist challenge divided and in disarray.	United, there is little we cannot do in a host of new joint ventures. Divided there is little we can do—for we dare not meet a powerful foe at odds and split asunder.

STEVENSON	SORENSEN
if the free way of life doesn't help the many poor of this world it will never save the few rich.	If freedom's way cannot help the many who are poor, it can never save the few who are rich.
I would like to see permanent joint commissions at work . . . to undertake interstellar exploration, to conquer the deserts and tap the riches of the oceans . . .	Together let us explore the stars, conquer the deserts, . . . tap the ocean depths . . .

GALBRAITH	SORENSEN
the work of this new Administration will not be over in a hundred days, or in five hundred days, or in a thousand days. Its work will continue without surcease for all of the next four years.	All this will not be finished in the first one hundred days. Nor will it be finished in the first one thousand days, nor in the life of this Administration, nor even perhaps in our lifetime on this planet.
We will help these countries do so not as a part of an ideological struggle, not because they are pawns in a cold war, not to buy friendship. We will help them because to do so is right.	we pledge our best efforts to help you help yourselves, for whatever period is required— not because our enemies are doing it, not because we seek your votes, but because it is right.
We shall never negotiate out of fear. But we shall never fear to negotiate.	Let us never negotiate out of fear. But let us never fear to negotiate.

In addition to those contributions they had solicited, Kennedy and Sorensen also received suggestions from many others, none of which they seem to have used. These included a proposed peroration from *Washington Post* publisher Philip Graham and three points from the author (and Jacqueline Kennedy relative) Gore Vidal.*

*The cover letter to the Graham draft peroration, making reference to the immortal peroration of Lincoln's first inaugural, is in Sorensen's inaugural file in the Kennedy Library. Graham offered a draft, casting himself as William Seward to Kennedy's Abraham Lincoln. He noted that Lincoln's alchemy had actually converted an overwrought offering from Seward into classic prose:

SEWARD

I close. We are not, we must not be, aliens or enemies but fellow countrymen and brethren. Although passion has strained our bonds of affection too hardly, they must not, I am sure they will not be broken. The mystic chords which, proceeding from so many battle fields and so many patriot graves, pass through all the hearts and all the hearths in this broad continent of ours, will yet again harmonize in their ancient music when breathed upon by the guardian angel of the nation.

LINCOLN

I am loth to close. We are not enemies, but friends. We must not be enemies. Though passion may have strained, it must not break our bonds of affection. The mystic chords of memory, stretching from every battle-field, and patriot grave, to every living heart and hearthstone, all over this broad land, will yet swell the chorus of the Union, when again touched, as surely they will be, by the better angels of our nature.

I obtained a copy of the three-page draft itself from Graham's estate on the condition that it not be quoted, but it bears no relation to the final speech or any draft. Vidal's suggestions came in a letter he wrote to Kennedy on November 14, 1960, a copy of which Vidal sent to Sorensen. It argued for references to what became the Peace Corps, to the exploration of space (for which, as made clear in the text, the only actual reference was drawn from the Stevenson draft), and the broad subject of alienation. Other unsolicited and unused submissions included those from Louis Seltzer, editor of the *Cleveland Press*, Stevenson aide John Sharon, and Stevenson associate James Warburg.

On January 10, the day after the Massachusetts speech, aboard his plane the *Caroline*—the first jet ever chartered by a presidential candidate—Kennedy reviewed the TCS Draft and dictated to Mrs. Lincoln his own most significant contributions to his inaugural address. Mrs. Lincoln's typescript of the dictation she took has been lost, but a full transcription of the shorthand—the first ever published—is reproduced below as Appendix C.

The dictation makes clear that Kennedy was prepared to accept the bulk of the TCS Draft; he seems to have instructed Mrs. Lincoln to take in its "p. 3, 4, 5" and some or all of page six wholesale. But there was also new material Kennedy wished to add, and flashes of pessimism from the TCS Draft (*the worst is fast upon us, a globe hell-bent for planned or accidental suicide*) were rejected at this juncture.

The new language Kennedy dictated, some form of which made it into the address, was the following:

- this generation was "born in this century—tempered by the war"
- "And we shall pay any price, bear any burden, meet any hardships, support any friend, oppose any foe . . ."
- "Since this country was founded, every generation of Americans has been called at least once to give testimony to their national loyalty. The graves of young Americans who responded circle [undecipherable] the globe."
- "Can we forge against these enemies, a great alliance North & South—East & West . . ."
- "A few generations has it been given—in the long history of the world [to] defend freedom at a time of maximum danger. I do not shrink from this responsibility—I welcome it. I do not believe we should change places with any other people or any other generations.
- "the glow in a fire would light the world."

Kennedy also both improved and added to the signature phrase emerging toward the conclusion of the speech:

TCS DRAFT	KENNEDY DICTATION
So ask not what your country is going to do for you. Ask what you can do for your country.	My fellow Americans, ask not what your country will do for you, ask rather what you can do for your country. My fellow citizens of the world, ask not what America or any other country will do for you, but rather what you yourself can do for freedom.

This was a very good day's work for a writer—it actually came at the end of a long day, filled with other tasks—and marks a major contribution to the evolution of the inaugural address. But it is also important to note that the Kennedy dictation was not truly the next draft of the inaugural address. It includes a possible new beginning—speaking of Kennedy's predecessors in the presidency, and referring to each of the first five of them by name—that never seems to have been considered again. It also includes an elaborate nautical metaphor (*we set sail today on seas on subterranean explosions . . . we sail with high confidence in the fixed stars*) that also seems to have vanished without a trace.

Instead it is clear that the TCS Draft remained the working version of the speech, informed by contributions from the Kennedy dictation, just as Sorensen's earlier work had been informed (indeed, highlighted) by contributions from Stevenson, Galbraith, and perhaps Nevins and Kraft. It is simply not correct to say, as a recent book did, that, with the Kennedy dictation, the speech became "in every important respect" Kennedy's own handiwork. In fact, of the fifty-one sentences in the inaugural address, John Kennedy might be said to have been the principal original author of no more than fourteen. And this number credits Kennedy with every sentence the origin of which is unclear. On direct evidence—the dictation and the changes made at the time of delivery—only nine sentences were principally originally Kennedy's. This compares with eight sentences from Adlai Stevenson.

As Sorensen observed in a lecture he gave at Columbia University in the spring of 1963 (of which Kennedy wrote the foreword to the published version):

> . . . group authorship is rarely, if ever, successful. A certain continuity and precision of style, and unity of argument, must be carefully drafted, particularly in a public communication that will be read or heard by many diverse audiences. Its key principles and phrases can be debated, outlined, and later reviewed by a committee, but basically authorship depends on one man alone with his typewriter or pen. (Had the Gettysburg address been written by a committee, its ten sentences would surely have grown to a hundred, its simple pledges would surely have been hedged, and the world would have indeed have little noted or long remembered what was said there.)

The point about "one man alone" is an overstatement, and Kennedy's inaugural appears to have been that rare successful collaboration. But if we must identify its "continuity and precision of style" with "one man," that man must surely be not John Kennedy but Theodore Sorensen.

∽ Sorensen clearly recalls receiving a telephone call from Kennedy during a brunch for the Kennedy cabinet held at the home of Labor Secretary–designate Arthur Goldberg on Sunday,

January 15. Kennedy called to discuss the inaugural address, and Sorensen took the call in the basement "rec room." It is the only extended telephone conversation Sorensen recalls with Kennedy about the speech.

On January 16, for the first time, Sorensen and Kennedy met in person to work on the speech.* The meeting occurred inside Joseph Kennedy's home in Palm Beach, and lasted from about 10:15 A.M. until perhaps 11:30.† This session likely began with the

---

*Sorensen's *Kennedy*, which is inaccurate on many of the details of this process, says that this meeting occurred on an oceanside patio, but Sorensen now insists that it was indoors. The chronology presented here is also at variance to that recalled by Evelyn Lincoln, Kennedy's personal secretary, in both her memoirs and in a memorandum she prepared in 1987 for Professor Vito Silvestri, and which Professor Silvestri generously shared with me. I have concluded that while Mrs. Lincoln's contemporaneous diaries and calendars are reliable, her later recollections simply are not. The 1987 Lincoln-Silvestri memorandum vividly recalls Kennedy dictating portions of the inaugural on December 28, 1960 (including the "ask not" passage), and January 15, 1961. But Mrs. Lincoln's 1965 book, *My Twelve Years with John F. Kennedy*, makes no reference to the ostensible December 28 dictation, although she correctly recalls the same passage being dictated on a flight that took place January 10. And Mrs. Lincoln's 1987 recollection of the ostensible January 15 dictation of the inaugural includes a specific reference to Kennedy's concern about having recently gained weight ("My God . . . if I don't lose five pounds this week we might have to call off the inauguration") that her contemporaneous diaries place on January 16—and in connection with dictating routine correspondence, not the inaugural address. This latter confusion likely began when Mrs. Lincoln wrote her book, in which she also placed Kennedy's complaint about his weight on January 15 rather than January 16. Thurston Clarke's recent *Ask Not* fails to distinguish between the reliability of Mrs. Lincoln's contemporary notes and the frequent fallibility of her later recollections. Clarke also fails to note any of these inconsistencies.

†11:30 A.M. is my estimate. Mrs. Lincoln's contemporaneous diary entry for January 16 indicates that following the Kennedy-Sorensen session, and before going off at 12:45 P.M. to change before lunch and golf with Senator George Smathers and Reverend Billy Graham, Kennedy gave an interview to Laura Bergquist of *Look* magazine and took telephone calls from Sargent and Eunice Shriver, Senator Albert Gore, and Senator James Eastland.

shortened version of the TCS Draft (reproduced in Appendix B) and the Kennedy dictation before the two men. When it ended, Sorensen typed up another draft. Laura Bergquist, a reporter for *Look* magazine in Palm Beach to write the text accompanying a photo essay by Richard Avedon on Jacqueline and Caroline Kennedy, was the president-elect's next appointment after Sorensen. She later recalled that, as she and Kennedy talked, "Out by the pool Ted Sorensen sat at a typewriter, pecking away at a new draft of the inaugural speech."

Kennedy and Sorensen reconvened the next morning on Joseph Kennedy's patio to polish the new draft. That work continued as they left Palm Beach aboard Kennedy's Convair for Washington. By the time the plane landed, the two men had produced the penultimate draft of the address.*

But the flight on the *Caroline* that day is most notable for giving rise to a historic misunderstanding—Sorensen at first labels it a "fraud," though he then hastens to add that that is too strong a word—about an apparent "version" of the inaugural address in John Kennedy's own hand.

At one point during the flight, having completed editing the speech with Sorensen, and with a typed draft before him, Kennedy asked Evelyn Lincoln for a yellow legal pad and, beginning above the first line on the sheet, wrote the words "what your country is going to do for you—ask what you can do for your country." Above the first of these words, in the empty space at the top of sheet, he then added the words "ask not," so that it

---

*What I call the penultimate draft, reproduced in Appendix D, is the typescript version of a draft found in Kennedy's inaugural file, with a carbon copy found in Sorensen's. I have favored the typescript over the many (and sometimes differing) handwritten corrections to both Kennedy's copy and Sorensen's carbon, as the corrections are necessarily subsequent to the typescript.

read "ask not what your country is going to do for you—ask what you can do for your country." He then wrote another three sentences. As Sorensen now recalls, Kennedy placed this single sheet in a compartment or drawer of the plane's desk, noting with a wink that he had read recently that part of an FDR inaugural in Roosevelt's hand had sold for hundreds of thousands of dollars. Kennedy suggested to Sorensen that perhaps he had just created a piece of memorabilia from which his own family might someday similarly profit.

It appears, however, that either before beginning or after completing his work with Sorensen, Kennedy extended the prank. In front of on-board interviewer Hugh Sidey of *Time* magazine, he read over three full pages he had just committed to the legal pad.

> "It's tough," mused Jack Kennedy. "The speech to the Massachusetts legislature went so well. It's going to be hard to meet that standard." He read the three pages aloud, ticking off historical allusions. He paused for a moment, then murmured some doubts about the long introductory part of the speech. "What I want to say," he explained, "is that the spirit of the revolution still is here, still is a part of this country." He wrote for a minute or two, crossed out a few words, then flung the tablet on the desk and began talking over a wide variety of subjects.

By the time the flight had ended, Kennedy had scrawled across nine legal pad sheets, of which the one done in front of Sorensen became the last, the ones read to Sidey the first, and five more in between. Taken together, these have been presented publicly as "an early draft of the inaugural speech." The legal pad sheets contain many cross-outs, interlineations, and incomplete sentences, all seemingly the hallmarks of an early draft. In fact, the inaugural address had already been essentially completed, and, as Sorensen notes, this memorabilia version "had absolutely nothing to do with the evolution of the speech." A transcription—the first ever published—of the complete "memorabilia version," which Kennedy, with a flourish, hand-dated "January 17, 1961," is reproduced in Appendix F. Surprisingly, the handwritten version almost perfectly copies out the dictation Kennedy had related to Mrs. Lincoln one week earlier. In fact, so similar are the two versions that it seems almost a certainty that Kennedy had a typescript of the dictation at hand when he created the "memorabilia version." No such typescript survives.

This creation of a holographic version "proving" Kennedy's authorship of the speech is reminiscent of the paper trail for *Profiles in Courage*. Herbert Parmet wrote of Kennedy's handwritten notes for that book: "They indicate very rough passages without paragraphing, without any shape, largely ideas jotted down as possible sections, obviously necessitating editing. That portion of the handwritten material . . . in no way resembles the final product." Thurston Clarke calls the inaugural manuscript "a charade, but an honorable one, performed to reinforce the truth" that Kennedy was "in every important respect" the author of the speech. But this makes no sense, on several levels. First, as a matter of normal human behavior, people do not undertake elaborate charades to prove that which is already true (especially when it has not yet been denied). Second, Kennedy, as Parmet concludes, seems to have undertaken such a charade before, and not for noble purposes. Finally, as we have seen, the January 10 dictation, which forms the basis for Clarke's claim of Kennedy's authorship of the speech "in every important respect," establishes no such thing. Perhaps Kennedy expected that all drafts prior to the dictation (such as the TCS Draft) would be destroyed; in fact, no such copies remained in anyone's files—except his own.

Asked if Kennedy's intent with the handwritten draft might have been to create a documentary record of authorship of the speech, Sorensen notes that "he had been challenged about the authorship of *Profiles in Courage,* and he went to some lengths to provide a documentary record of authorship, showing people handwritten pages which, possibly, had been created for that purpose. Maybe he was doing it again. I don't know."

Within a few months after the inauguration, the White House released a photo of the first page of the "memorabilia version," the page bearing the date, to the editors of a book on the Kennedy Administration's first hundred days. The caption of the photo read, "The President's first draft of the inaugural address."

∽ While Sorensen remained in Washington on January 17, Kennedy flew later the same evening to New York, arriving in the city just after midnight. It was the evening of President Eisenhower's farewell address to the nation warning of a "military-industrial complex" and also the same day that a key speech by Nikita Khrushchev on "wars of national liberation" was first published in the West. The president-elect spent Wednesday the 18th at New York's Carlyle Hotel, having his clothes fitted for the inauguration, visiting his dentist—and possibly engaging in an assignation.

Sorensen, in Washington, was meanwhile polishing the speech, supervising the many changes that separate the penultimate draft from Kennedy's reading copy. Sorensen took the penultimate draft to Walter Lippmann's house, where he had lunch with Lippmann and sat while the columnist read the speech over. Lippmann suggested at least one change: referring to the Soviet bloc not as "those nations that would make themselves our *enemy*" but as "those nations that would make themselves our *adversary.*"

Sorensen, and later Kennedy, found this phrasing so superior that they adopted it for the inaugural, and repeatedly thereafter.* Other than that, Lippmann made "a few rhetorical suggestions," the details of which neither he nor Sorensen could later recall. In any event, Lippmann considered the draft nearly finished. "All of the famous Sorensen chiliastic turns of speech were there."

Incoming Secretary of State Dean Rusk read the draft and suggested that "fellow citizens of the world" be enjoined to ask not "what you can do for freedom" but "what together we can do for the freedom of man." Washington attorney Clark Clifford may have reviewed the draft at this point. Galbraith came by Sorensen's office in the afternoon and suggested a number of other editorial changes, particularly in the phrasing of those paragraphs addressed to Third World nations.

Finally, following Kennedy's return to Washington and a forty-five-minute meeting between Kennedy and Sorensen to review these changes and make others, the reading copy was produced. By 7:15 that Wednesday evening, January 18, the speech was essentially finished. From sometime not long after that, Kennedy had the reading copy with him at nearly all times until he delivered the address on Friday. A hold-for-release version for the press corps was also produced from the same text by Press Secretary Pierre Salinger's Kennedy Press Office; it noted: "There should be no premature release of this speech, nor should its contents be paraphrased, alluded to or hinted at in earlier stories."

At some point on Thursday, however, Sorensen decided to seek two changes in the speech, both dealing with the issue of

---

*Twenty-two subsequent Kennedy uses of "adversary" include passages in Kennedy's Special Message (second State of the Union) of May 25, 1961, his address to the United Nations of September 25, 1961, and his American University speech of June 10, 1963.

The last page of the Memorabilia version of the inaugural, in Kennedy's handwriting and dated (on its first page) January 17, 1961. Sorensen notes that "he had been challenged about the authorship of *Profiles in Courage*, and he went to some lengths to provide a documentary record of authorship, showing handwritten pages which possibly had been created for that purpose. Maybe he was doing it again. I don't know." The words are: "ask not what your country is going to do for you—ask what you can do for your country—My fellow citizens of the world, ask not what America or others will do for you—Ask rather what you [give for] can do for freedom. Ask of us the same high standards of sacrifice and strength of heart and soul that we seek from you." [John F. Kennedy Library] civil rights in the United States. The two suggested changes were typed up on a sheet given to Kennedy marked "CHANGES IN IN-AUGURAL SPEECH—TO BE READ AND APPROVED BY SENATOR."

The changes were suggested by Kennedy civil rights aides Harris Wofford and Louis Martin, who noted with great unhappiness that the entire address dealt with foreign affairs and that civil rights had not been mentioned at all. Why not, they asked, append to the language about "those human rights to which this nation has been committed, and to which we are committed today" the additional words "at home and around the world"? Sorensen had once helped found what became the Lincoln, Nebraska, chapter of the Congress of Racial Equality, and had testified as a young man before the Nebraska legislature in favor of Fair Employment Practices. He agreed with Wofford and Martin. So did Kennedy, and the five additional words were typed onto his reading copy. As the press had already been given the speech, this addition (and those less substantive changes Kennedy extemporized) quickly became well known.

What did not become known was a second, far more important change that Sorensen suggested at the same time. Following the rhetorical question, "Will you join in that historic effort?" it was proposed to add the following: "*Are you willing to demonstrate in your own life—in your attitude toward those of other races and those here from other shores—that you hold these truths to be self-evident?*"

This would have been perhaps the most dramatic presidential statement on race relations ever made in the United States. Kennedy declined to add it to his speech. Sorensen, whose own first nationally published article—in 1952 in *The New Republic*—had been a call for racial integration, does not recall why. Wofford now gives conflicting accounts, acknowledging authorship in one interview while saying in another that he does not recall even being aware that the language had been proposed, disclaiming authorship of the line and saying it "sounds like Ted."

2

Why

No great speech is written in a vacuum. The historical and literary context for John Kennedy's inaugural address is an essential element to a full understanding of the speech and how it came to be written.

The historical context included a particular outlook on the world, and America's place in it, shared by John Kennedy and much of his generation. They were men of the postwar, junior officers during the Second World War—a description that fit both Nixon and Kennedy—and now succeeding their senior officers, most notably Eisenhower and his circle, who had come to political power at war's end. Their worldview began with the salience of foreign policy issues in preference to domestic concerns, for they believed that foreign policy failures, chiefly culminating at Munich, had brought on the war, and that foreign policy successes, chiefly the Marshall Plan, NATO, and the Truman Doctrine, had preserved the "hard and bitter peace." If political consultants had dominated either party's leading circles in 1960—as they did not yet do—their mantra would certainly have been "It's the cold war, stupid."

And the view of the cold war that informed both candidates' strategies was a curious mix of optimism and pessimism: optimism about America and its productive capacity, but a heartfelt fear of an emerging Soviet behemoth, thought to be efficient, disciplined, and fanatically determined. Overlaying all of this, moreover, was a real sense of the imminence of possible nuclear holocaust—just fifteen years into the atomic age—nuclear weapons having already proven decisive in one military theater (Japan in 1945) and having been forgone in perhaps only one or two others (Korea in 1950 and possibly Indochina in 1954).

More specifically, a handful of books, most of them published in the years just before the inaugural, seem to have played a large role in shaping both Kennedy's and Sorensen's thinking—and their prose.

The most important substantive decision in crafting the speech, of course, was to limit it to foreign policy, to avoid domestic issues altogether (and then, when challenged on this, to make just a three-word allusion to civil rights). At his first press conference as president—the first presidential press conference ever televised live—Kennedy was questioned on this very point:

Q: Mr. President, your inaugural address was unusual in that you dealt only with America's position in the world. Why, Mr. President, did you limit yourself to this global theme?

A: Well, because the issue of war and peace is involved, and the survival of perhaps the planet, possibly our system. And, therefore, this is a matter of primary concern to the people of the United States and the people of the world. Secondly, I represent a new administration. I think the views of this administration are quite well known to the American people, and will become better known in the next month. I think that we are new, however, on the world scene, and therefore I felt there would be some use in informing countries around the world of our general view on the questions which face the world and divide the world.

The second of these two points is disingenuous on its face, however. There is no reason to believe that the views of the Kennedy administration on domestic issues were better "known to the American people" than those on international affairs. Indeed, the campaign debates had focused, to an unusual degree, on foreign policy—as had Kennedy's pre-presidential experience.

In the years since the address, Kennedy's critics have suggested he omitted domestic policy from the inaugural for the same reason that he came only belatedly to the struggle for civil rights. Thus Henry Fairlie has written, "We must remember that John Kennedy had excised any mention of domestic issues from the inaugural address because they tend to divide; it was in this manner that he conducted his administration."

But that is not quite right. Fairlie accurately pinpoints Walt Rostow's 1960 book, *The Stages of Economic Growth*, as an important influence on Kennedy's thinking at this time. Rostow, a professor of economic history at MIT, was a Kennedy campaign adviser, a contributor to the Galbraith drafts of the inaugural address, and had been named a White House staff aide on national security matters. Sorensen notes that Rostow is "generally credited" with the Kennedy campaign theme, "We've got to get this country moving again." In Senate speeches, Kennedy had adopted Rostow's analysis of the developing world. (Rostow was later to be transferred to the State Department, to head policy planning there.)

What Fairlie fails to note, however, is that Rostow's book, subtitled *A Non-Communist Manifesto*, declared a sort of end of history with respect to domestic policy questions in the United States.

Rostow asked,

> Leave aside the arms race and the threat of war, and consider this question: what lies beyond? What will happen to societies when income provides such good food for virtually all that it raises questions of public health by its very richness; where housing is of an order that people are not tempted to exert themselves much to improve it; where clothing is similarly adequate; where a Lambretta or Volkswagen is within the grasp of virtually all—if not necessarily a twin-tailed American monster? This stage has not yet been fully attained; but it has been attained by enough of the American and Northern European population to pose, as a serious and meaningful problem, the nature of the next stage.

What Rostow saw ahead was pervasive suburban boredom, though he allowed that "the exploration of outer space [might] offer an adequately interesting and expensive outlet for resources and ambitions."

But Kennedy envisioned the hole in this doughnut of prosperity: "leave aside the arms race and the threat of war." *That was the issue of the 1960s.* Domestic questions were not worth addressing *not* because they were divisive (that would come later) but because they were all but resolved; simply, from a historical perspective, unimportant. Looking backward, we see Kennedy and Nixon disagreeing on domestic policies, ranging from civil rights to the role of government in health care and housing. But from the vantage point of January 1961, Kennedy saw these differences as tactical and transitory. What we see as a cold war consensus, as sideshow debates on the Chinese threat to the coastal islands of Quemoy and Matsu, he saw as fundamental philosophical differences on the only real issue of the day that mattered—how much strength was necessary to meet the challenge posed by the Soviet Union. And the presidency, as had long been understood, was at its zenith in confronting such issues. Alexis de Toqueville had long ago noted that "It is chiefly in foreign relations that the executive power of a nation finds occasion to exert its skill and strength." Viewed through this lens, the focus of the inaugural address on international relations alone is not just logical but inevitable.

Rostow's analysis of economic growth stages carried with it both a description of how the Soviet Union had come to adopt an aggressive posture in foreign policy as well as a prescription for how that challenge should be met, particularly in the Third World.[*]

The Soviets, Rostow argued, had made the choice all nations face at the point of economic "takeoff": between the "temptations of power"—nationalism deployed to redress past humiliations, pursue future aggrandizement, or simply consolidate political control—and the "blandishments of high mass consumption"—nationalism deployed in aid of modernization.

With the Soviets having made this choice, the battleground, Rostow now maintained, shifted to two arenas, the military sphere and the Third World. Kennedy's speech took a similar view. The task for the West, and especially for the United States, was threefold:

- That it not permit the Soviets to get far enough ahead in an arms race "to make a temporary military solution rational" (*We dare not tempt them with weakness.*)

---

[*]The phrase "Third World," originally from the French (and a play on "Third Estate"), was coined in the 1950s. It did not appear in the Oxford English Dictionary until 1963 (or in Rostow's book) but was used in English as early as 1958.

- To move the Third World toward economic "takeoff," through "a partnership which will see them through into sustained growth," "resisting the blandishments and temptations of Communism. This is," Rostow wrote, "the single most important item on the Western agenda." "The problem lies not in the mysterious East, but in the inscrutable West." (*We shall always hope to find them strongly supporting their own freedom. . . . We pledge our best efforts to help them help themselves. . . . We offer a special pledge—to convert our good words into good deeds—in a new alliance for progress—to assist free men and free governments in casting off the chains of poverty.*)
- To "demonstrate to Russians that there is an interesting and lively alternative for Russia on the world scene to either an arms race or unconditional surrender." (*So let us begin anew. . . . Let both sides explore what problems unite us. . . . Let both sides seek to invoke the wonders of science. . . . Let both sides join in creating a new endeavor, not a new balance of power, but a new world of law.*)

As these points and phrases remind us, Kennedy wished to send two distinct messages to the Soviets: like the eagle in the Great Seal of the United States, Kennedy held out both the olive branch and the arrows.

Of these, the confrontational language was by far the less controversial. Thus the National Intelligence Estimate of December 1, 1960, had declared that "There is no evidence at present to indicate that the Soviets will come to accept a world system which assumes the genuine coexistence of states and ideologies." And: "This is what the Soviets mean by 'peaceful coexistence'— a strategy to defeat the West without war."

Nikita Khrushchev, Kennedy's adversary, was a showman, veering constantly from bluster to menace. For fully twenty-five days, in September and October 1960—at the height of an American presidential campaign—he had held forth in residence at the United Nations General Assembly in New York, cavorting with Fidel Castro in Harlem, banging his shoe on the table at the UN. In his opening statement in the first presidential debate with Nixon, Kennedy had taken note of this: "Mr. Khrushchev is in New York, and he maintains the Communist offensive throughout the world because of the productive power of the Soviet Union itself." The same National Intelligence Estimate held that Soviet GNP was growing twice as fast as U.S. GNP.

On January 6, 1961, just as Kennedy and Sorensen were turning their attention to the composition of the inaugural address, Khrushchev gave a speech of his own seeming to confirm American estimates of his intentions. Over the strong opposition of the Chinese Communists, Khrushchev indicated that he was prepared to negotiate with the United States and its allies and to pursue "peaceful coexistence." But at the same time Khrushchev emphasized his commitment to support "wars of national liberation or popular uprisings" of "colonial peoples against their oppressors." "Communists are revolutionaries," he said, "and it would be a bad thing if they did not exploit new opportunities." The Khrushchev speech was published on January 17. The National Intelligence Estimate of that date stated: "It is one of the key points in the Soviet estimate of the world situation that conditions are favorable for Communist gains in the colonial and ex-colonial areas of the world; there is much to support this Soviet view."

The Khrushchev speech was not published in English translation until January 18 and thus came to Kennedy's attention only after he had completed work on the inaugural. But the questions it posed were clear, and widely recognized. On the morning of the inauguration, the *New York Times* published an editorial on the subject entitled "Challenge to a New President." The *Times* called the speech Khrushchev's "contribution to the inauguration of a new American President" and suggested that it was "obviously designed to set the terms for the negotiations he seeks with Mr. Kennedy."

In the West, Khrushchev's threats were taken even more seriously than, in retrospect, they should have been. "There was no reason why the United States should fear for its security in 1960," Henry Fairlie has written, "yet this fear consumed the press . . . and it informed almost every major speech which John Kennedy made during his campaign. . . ." In fact, Kennedy had not just played on such fears, he had shared them, and for twenty years, since he had personally observed the British government's failed appeasement of Hitler.

The modern interpretation of the failure of this policy—Prime Minister Neville Chamberlain's defeat at Munich—is that Britain lacked the will to fight. By 1945, as he considered entering politics, Kennedy had adopted this view as well. But in 1940, in *Why England Slept*, the book that grew out of his Harvard senior thesis, Kennedy had argued that Chamberlain had made the only decision possible at Munich, the "realistic" decision, because Britain was by then so badly overmatched by German military capability. In *Why England Slept*, Kennedy had written that the key British failure had come earlier, around 1935, in the decision not to rearm sooner.

Democracies, he argued, are slow to respond to potential threats.

A dictatorship's leaders realize that ordinarily armaments are so repugnant to a democracy based on a capitalistic system—which means everything must be paid for from taxes—that it will get along on a minimum armament program. A democracy will merely try to counter-balance the menaces that are actually staring it in the face.

Democracy is the superior form of government, because it is based on a respect for man as a reasonable being. *For the long run*, then, democracy is superior. But for the short run, democracy has great weaknesses. When it competes with a system of government which cares nothing for permanency, a system built primarily for war, democracy, which is built primarily for peace, is at a disadvantage.

Democracies require "voluntary action and co-operation," Kennedy wrote as a student. "But you cannot get efficient voluntary action in a democracy unless people feel that sacrifices are essential." Twenty years later, as he began his race for the presidency, the insight endured—but now Kennedy began to see himself as able to solve the problem:

A free society is at a disadvantage in competing against an organized, monolithic state such as Russia. We prize our individualism and rightly so, but we need a cohesive force. In America that force is the presidency.

In January 1961, then, when Kennedy saw freedom "in its hour of maximum danger," he did not shrink from the responsibilities of the presidency, he welcomed them. The office provided the only platform on which, he believed, salvation could be built.

᨞ The nuclear nightmare pervades Kennedy's inaugural.

The speech begins with the observation that "man holds in his mortal hands the power to abolish all forms of human poverty and all forms of human life," continues with the thought that "the instruments of war have outpaced the instruments of peace," and warns that "the dark powers of destruction unleashed by science" threaten to "engulf all humanity in planned or accidental self-destruction" while "both sides" are "racing to alter that uncertain balance of terror that stays the hand of mankind's final war." For Kennedy, especially having watched Europe in 1938–1939 plunge into the abyss fewer than twenty years after the War to End All Wars, this nightmare was very real. It was a vision with which he had been contending since his first days in politics.

It was also at the heart of a policy debate in which the country was engaged in 1959, 1960, and 1961. Just as Rostow's *Stages of Economic Growth* had set out a framework for much of Kennedy foreign policy, another book, Maxwell Taylor's *The Uncertain Trumpet*, set the terms of debate for Kennedy on military policy. Taylor, a four-star general, had been army chief of staff from 1955 to 1959. Considered for a number of roles in the new administration, he was named the president's chief military adviser in mid-1961. Kennedy later named him chairman of the Joint Chiefs and may have intended this eventual appointment from the outset.

The Uncertain Trumpet, published shortly after Taylor's 1959 retirement from the army, continued in public an argument that Taylor had been conducting in private (and before a congressional subcommittee chaired by Lyndon Johnson) with other members of the Joint Chiefs. Taylor advocated a new military doctrine of "flexible response" while his colleagues preferred to continue with the established policy of "massive retaliation." Taylor enjoyed important academic support, including the old sage George Kennan and the rising star Henry Kissinger. Sorensen recalls that "JFK was very impressed" by *The Uncertain Trumpet*.

"Massive retaliation" made the nation's nuclear deterrent effectively both its first and last line of defense against the Soviets. It postulated that the principal Soviet threat was itself nuclear, but that even a conventional military challenge by the Soviets—such as a cutoff of Berlin—could be deterred by the threat of a massive nuclear strike. "Flexible response," on the other hand, was premised on the notion that smaller challenges—"limited wars"—were becoming more prevalent, and that a threat of nuclear retaliation against a Soviet move in, say, the Congo, Laos, or Vietnam was so out of scale as to be literally incredible.

Accordingly, Taylor sought to "expose the Great Fallacy that Massive Retaliation is an all-weather, all-purpose strategy which is adequate to cope with any military challenge." One motivation for "massive retaliation" had been that nuclear weapons were economical, literally less expensive in dollar terms than the conventional arms it was asserted they could replace. Kennedy and Taylor believed that Eisenhower had economized to a fault, however, resulting also in a "missile gap" in nuclear weapons. This related critique was championed by another general-turned-author, James Gavin, in a 1958 book entitled *War and Peace in the Space Age*. But Gavin's argument, while politically explosive, was about tactical issues, such as how many missiles were needed to ensure second-strike capability. Taylor was a strategist.

Military policy objectives, Taylor argued, must be aligned with political and economic ends; such actions "should be taken to the sure notes of a certain trumpet, giving to friend or foe alike a clear expression of our purpose and our motives." A buildup of conventional (and perhaps tactical nuclear) arms would be required, but this was necessary to secure the peace. *Only when our arms are sufficient beyond doubt can we be certain beyond doubt that they will never be employed.*

ᔓ Style, of course, was every bit as crucial to the success of the speech as substance. And the Kennedy-Sorensen style was also heavily influenced by the intellectual currents of the late 1950s and early 1960s.

In 1957, E. B. White wrote an article for *The New Yorker* beginning, "A small book arrived in my mail not long ago, a gift from a friend in Ithaca. It is *The Elements of Style*, by the late William Strunk, Jr., and it was known on the Cornell campus in my day as 'the little book,' with the stress on the word 'little.'" White had not seen Strunk's volume for thirty-eight years; Strunk had died in 1946, and the book had long been out of print, having been replaced, White mourned, by "books with upswept tail fins and automatic verbs." But now he rediscovered it with delight, enchanting and intriguing the readers of his magazine. "Boldness," White wrote, was perhaps Strunk's book's "chief distinguishing mark."

By 1959, Macmillan had reissued "the little book" "with revisions, an introduction and a new chapter on writing" by White. "Strunk" (it was not yet "Strunk and White") quickly became the handbook for a new generation of writers, including Theodore Sorensen, then a member of Kennedy's Senate and campaign staff, who obtained a copy in 1959 and "thought it was brilliant." Sorensen speculates that he may have received his copy from Joseph Kraft.

Among Strunk's watchwords:

- "use the active voice"
- writing that is briefer is "more forcible," "brevity is a by-product of vigor"
- "avoid fancy words"*

---

*As Sorensen wrote, Kennedy "used little or no slang, dialect, legalistic terms, contractions, clichés, elaborate metaphors or ornate figures of speech. . . . The intellectual level of his speeches showed erudition but not arrogance."

- "avoid foreign languages"
- "place the emphatic words of a sentence at the end"

Most important of all was the lesson Sorensen later found also in the great speeches of Lincoln: "*Omit needless words.*"

> Vigorous writing is concise. A sentence should contain no unnecessary words, a paragraph no unnecessary sentences, for the same reason that a drawing should have no unnecessary lines and a machine no unnecessary parts. This requires not that the writer make all his sentences short, or that he avoid all detail and treat his subjects only in outline, but that every word tell.

When later summing up the Kennedy-Sorensen style—"our style and standard increasingly became one"—Sorensen implicitly acknowledged this debt:

> We were not conscious of following the elaborate techniques later ascribed to these speeches by literary analysts. Neither of us had any special training in composition, linguistics or semantics. Our chief criterion was always audience comprehension and comfort, and this meant: (1) short speeches, short clauses and short words, whenever possible; (2) a series of points or propositions in numbered or logical sequence, whenever appropriate; and (3) the construction of sentences, phrases and paragraphs in such a manner as to simplify, clarify and emphasize.

∽ If Strunk was Kennedy and Sorensen's model editor, Lincoln himself was almost certainly the writer they most sought to emulate. Debating Senator Douglas, Lincoln had said that Douglas "confused a similarity of words with a similarity of things—as one might equate a horse chestnut with a chestnut horse." Lincoln would have done no such thing. As his partner William Herndon noted long ago, and as Garry Wills has stressed more recently, Lincoln considered word choice a painstaking task. "He would have agreed with Mark Twain that the difference between the right word and the nearly right one is that between the lightning and the lightning bug." The evolution of Kennedy's inaugural address, up through and including the many word changes made on delivery, are testimony to a similar focus.

Kennedy and Sorensen drew on sources well beyond Lincoln for inspiration, however. Myer Feldman recalls Sorensen reading Pericles' Funeral Oration in preparation for his work on the inaugural, and Sorensen says, "I think I probably did read it. I am sure JFK read it first." The inaugural did not refer to Pericles—though Kennedy's January 9 speech to the Massachusetts Legislature did—but the echoes are clear:

- "I will speak first of our ancestors." *I have sworn before you and Almighty God the same solemn oath our forebears prescribed nearly a century and three quarters ago.*
- "I should like to point out by what principles of action we rose to power, and under what institutions and through what manner of life our empire became great." *Born in this century, tempered by war, disciplined by a hard and bitter peace, proud of our ancient heritage . . .*
- "Our government does not copy our neighbors', but is an example to them." *We dare not forget today that we are the heirs of that first revolution.*
- "We alone do good to our neighbors not upon a calculation of interest, but in the confidence of freedom, and in a frank and fearless spirit." *Not because the communists may be doing it, not because we seek their votes, but because it is right.*

On a much more modern note, the author Richard Reeves has said that Winston Churchill was the inspiration for Kennedy's prose, but this is not quite right. Reeves cites Kennedy's *Why England Slept*, published in 1940, the title of which was a play on Churchill's *While England Slept* from 1938. But it was Arthur Krock of the *New York Times*, a friend of Joseph Kennedy's, who devised the title for the twenty-three-year-old John Kennedy's book, and it is simply not the case that *Why England Slept* was "a thin companion volume" to Churchill's book. *While England Slept* is a collection of Winston Churchill's speeches from 1932 to 1938, assembled by his son Randolph. The last speech in the book was delivered in March 1938, more than five months before Munich. *Why England Slept*, a narrative, begins by posing the question, "Why was England so poorly prepared for the war?" Kennedy did not begin writing it until September 1939, after the war had broken out, and it was not published until July 1940, months after the fall of France, to which it refers. Some of Churchill's ideas clearly influenced Kennedy, but the young son of America's isolationist ambassador exhibits far more sympathy for Chamberlain than Churchill did, and the literary style of the two volumes is very different, as a narrative of recent history and a collection of speeches must be.

Reeves also claims that Kennedy's second book, *Profiles in Courage*, was "an American version" of Churchill's *Great Contemporaries*. Both books begin, Reeves says, with meditations on courage, the "first in human qualities because it is the quality that guarantees all others," according to Churchill; "the most admirable of human virtues" in the words of Kennedy.

But *Great Contemporaries* was also a collection of essays, in this case biographical in nature, which Churchill published between 1929 and 1937. Of the nineteen men portrayed in the original edition, only thirteen were British; Marshals Foch and Hindenburg were also included, as was Hitler. Indeed, while all the essays in *Great Contemporaries* were about important figures with whom Churchill was acquainted—nearly half of them in politics, the military, or both—they were by no means all admiring.

Profiles in Courage, on the other hand, is not a series of portraits of men Kennedy had known—six of the eight men portrayed in the book died before he was born—but rather of "great predecessors," courageous figures in the history of the United States Senate. Moreover, *Profiles* derives its definition of courage—"grace under pressure"—not from Churchill but from Hemingway.

But Reeves is on to something. While Lincoln, not Churchill, was Kennedy's literary model, Churchill was without doubt the man from whom Kennedy sought to gain inspiration as a speaker. Arthur Schlesinger called Churchill Kennedy's "greatest admiration." Young John Kennedy had seen Churchill address the House of Commons in the run-up to the Second World War, and candidate Kennedy had listened to recordings of Churchill's wartime speeches when he sought to improve his own speaking ability. Kennedy well understood that, while writing and oratory are distinct talents, a truly great speech in the age of television would require these talents to converge.

3

How

Having described the process by which Kennedy's inaugural address was written, and the historical, policy, and literary context in which it was delivered, it remains to look closely at the words themselves.

Vice President Johnson, Mr. Speaker, Mr. Chief Justice, President Eisenhower, Vice President Nixon, President Truman, reverend clergy, fellow citizens

Kennedy began by singling out a number of dignitaries in the audience—Lyndon Johnson, the new vice president; Johnson's mentor, the elderly Speaker of the House Sam Rayburn; the chief justice, Earl Warren; the outgoing president, Dwight Eisenhower, and vice president, Richard Nixon; and the only other former president on hand, Harry Truman. (Presumably he would have mentioned Herbert Hoover as well, had Hoover's plane made it through the snowstorm.) Finally, he paid respect to the "reverend clergy." This beginning was almost certainly extemporized; the names were not included in Kennedy's large-print speech text, nor had there been any reference to them in any of the drafts of the address.

The formal address began with the words "fellow citizens." (Kennedy's first departure from the typescript came with the first word of the speech; he dropped the word "my" before "fellow citizens.")

This simple form of address was, in fact, deeply rooted in the history of the occasion. George Washington began the first inaugural address, on April 30, 1789, in New York City, with the salutation, "Fellow Citizens of the Senate and of the House of Representatives." At his second inaugural, on March 4, 1793, in Philadelphia, Washington simplified it to "Fellow Citizens." John Adams abjured any salutation whatever, but Thomas Jefferson reverted to Washington's phrase at his inaugural in 1801—the first to be held in the new capital city named for the first president. With that, nearly every president through Woodrow Wilson in 1917 began his inaugural by addressing his "fellow citizens."*

The Republican trio of Warren Harding, Calvin Coolidge, and Herbert Hoover preferred "My countrymen," and FDR varied his approach, but Harry Truman, a student of history, returned to Washington's salutation in 1949, and Eisenhower followed him in 1953 (though not 1957). Kennedy's choice of phrase was thus traditional.†

∽ *we observe today not a victory of party, but a celebration of freedom— symbolizing an end, as well as a beginning—signifying renewal, as well*

---

*The exceptions were James Madison, Zachary Taylor, Franklin Pierce, and one of the two addresses by each of Presidents Lincoln, Grant, and Wilson. In all, from Washington in 1789 through Wilson in 1917, twenty-five of thirty-three inaugurals began with the same phrase.

†The tradition continues; not since Jimmy Carter in 1977 has an inaugural address begun otherwise. "Fellow citizens" has been the salutation in thirty-six of fifty-five inaugurals to date.

as change. For I have sworn before you and Almighty God the same
solemn oath our forebears prescribed nearly a century and three quarters
ago.

The first substantive sentence of Kennedy's inaugural address
drew both on Winston Churchill and Woodrow Wilson. Addressing the V-E day crowd from the balcony of Britain's Min-
istry of Health on May 8, 1945, Churchill had declared, "This is
not a victory of party or of any class. It's a victory of the great
British nation as a whole." In his darkest days following near-
fatal spinal surgery in 1955, Kennedy passed the time copying out
and memorizing passages from Churchill's writing. Sorensen acknowledges that "both JFK and I loved Churchill" and that "it's
very possible that was the inspiration" for the opening phrase of
this sentence.

Woodrow Wilson's 1913 first inaugural, which Sorensen read
in preparation for his own work in 1961, was also a likely source.
Wilson began that speech with the simple words, "There has
been a change in government." But he went on, "It means much
more than the mere success of a party." And Wilson began his
peroration on the same note: "This is not a day of triumph; it is
a day of dedication. Here muster, not the forces of party, but the
forces of humanity." (It is worth recalling that Woodrow Wilson,
about whom Kennedy spoke often, was a more recent memory
for those in 1960–1961 than John Kennedy is for us today.)

While the opening portion of the TCS Draft has not sur-
vived, this first sentence is one of only four for which we have
the first draft of the speech. It began, "We celebrate today not a
victory of party but the sacrament of democracy—a ceremony
of peaceful change and renewal." By January 17, "sacrament of
democracy" had given way to "convention of freedom," and in
the two days thereafter "convention" became "celebration."

But the spirit of the original phrase, "sacrament of democracy," continues to pervade this first paragraph of the speech. As the sociologist Robert Bellah outlined in his landmark 1967 article of the name, Kennedy's inaugural address "serves as an example and a clue" to "Civil Religion in America." Bellah wrote, "The inauguration of a president is an important ceremonial event in this religion. It reaffirms, among other things, the religious legitimation of the highest political authority."*

Central to this undertaking is not only the presidential oath of office but a studied self-consciousness about the oath and its meaning. Of the forty-three inaugural addresses preceding Kennedy's, twenty-four made express reference to the oath of office and its sacred promise of service.† As Kennedy recognized, this reference to the oath just taken connects a new (or returning) president to all his predecessors, binding him in legitimacy to Washington, recalling to mind the legacy of Lincoln.

ဢ *The world is very different now. For man holds in his mortal hands the power to abolish all forms of human poverty and all forms of human life. And yet the same revolutionary beliefs for which our forebears fought are still at issue around the globe—the belief that the rights of man come not from the generosity of the state, but from the hand of God.*

*As Bellah notes, the phrase "civil religion" comes from Rousseau, and includes as precepts "the existence of God, the life to come, the reward of virtue and the punishment of vice, and the exclusion of religious intolerance."

†The line of such references began with Washington's second inaugural and ran through Madison (second), Monroe (second), John Quincy Adams, Jackson (second), Van Buren, William Henry Harrison, Polk, Taylor, Buchanan, Lincoln (both), Grant (first), Cleveland (both), Benjamin Harrison, McKinley (first), Taft, Wilson (second), Harding, Hoover, FDR (second and fourth), and Eisenhower (first).

The possibility of nuclear annihilation haunted, indeed obsessed John Kennedy from the outset of his political career. In his first partisan political address, his announcement speech for Congress in 1946, he observed that "we have a world which has unleashed the powers of atomic energy. We have a world capable of destroying itself." The nightmare never left him—and never strayed from the center of the political agenda as he saw it.

In Europe between the world wars he had wondered whether democracy was strong enough to survive the challenges of totalitarianism; it had been the central question in his undergraduate thesis, and then in his first book, *Why England Slept*. With the advent of nuclear weapons, this uncertainty took on apocalyptic overtones for Kennedy. Toward the end of his 1958 address to the annual dinner of Washington's Gridiron Club, Kennedy had said,

> The question is—whether a democratic society—with its freedom of choice—its breadth of opportunity—its range of alternatives—can meet the single-minded advance of the Communists. . . .
>
> Can a nation organized and governed as ours endure? That is the real question. Have we the nerve and the will? Have we got what it takes to carry through in an age where—as never before—our very survival is at stake—where we and the Russians have the power to destroy one-quarter of the earth's population—a feat not accomplished since Cain slew Abel?

In his 1960 Democratic National Convention acceptance speech, he repeated many of these words and then changed the arithmetic but continued with the same theme, noting that man "has taken into his mortal hands the power to exterminate the species some seven times over." This same challenge was the first Kennedy wished to pose in his inaugural address.

But Kennedy also wanted immediately to follow this glimpse into the abyss with a statement of his own credo, "*the belief that the rights of man come not from the generosity of the state, but from the hand of God.*" Sorensen says this was Kennedy's favorite "short-hand way to describe the difference between our system and totalitarian systems."

We dare not forget today that we are the heirs of that first revolution. Let the word go forth from this time and place, to friend and foe alike, that the torch has been passed to a new generation of Americans—born in this century, tempered by war, disciplined by a hard and bitter peace, proud of our ancient heritage—and unwilling to witness or permit the slow undoing of those human rights to which this Nation has always been committed, and to which we are committed today at home and around the world.

As with so much of Kennedy's inaugural, this memorable paragraph was not so much an original thought as a summing-up of what Kennedy had been saying—and hearing—for years.

In his speech nominating Adlai Stevenson for president at the Democratic National Convention in Chicago in 1956, Kennedy had said, "Let the word go forth that we have fulfilled our responsibility to the nation." The alliteration of "friend or foe" is actually a term with its origins in military jargon, and may specifically come from Maxwell Taylor's *Uncertain Trumpet*, a volume that, as we have seen, much influenced Kennedy's thinking. The final paragraph of Taylor's book begins, "All of the foregoing actions should be taken to the sure notes of a certain trumpet, giving to friend and foe alike a clear expression of our purpose and our motives."

The imagery of the passing of a torch likely stems from the relay preceding Olympiads, but as William Safire has observed,

The torch is a favorite political symbol. In 1555, just before being burned at the stake for heresy, English prelate Hugh Latimer said, "Be of good cheer, brother, we shall this day kindle such a torch in England as, I trust in God, shall never be extinguished."

In his introduction to *The Strategy of Peace*, a 1960 collection of Kennedy speeches, Allan Nevins had called the speeches of Theodore Roosevelt, Elihu Root, Woodrow Wilson, and Franklin Roosevelt "torches in the murk of their times" and said they were "worth reading still; they set standards which cannot be forgotten. We demand new torch-bearers, and we are getting them."

This is the first of two metaphorical references to fire in Kennedy's inaugural. Both hearken back to Washington's first inaugural and its declaration that "the sacred fire of liberty" has been "staked on the experiment entrusted to the hands of the American people." In fact, in the penultimate draft of Kennedy's speech "the torch" had been "the torch *of liberty.*"

The call to and on behalf of a "new generation of leadership" had been a staple of Kennedy's appeal since his first race for Congress in 1946, and its slogan that "The New Generation Offers a Leader." In a news conference on July 4, 1960, Kennedy had said, "It is time for a new generation of leadership to cope with new problems and new opportunities." The same month, in his speech accepting the presidential nomination, he had repeated, "It is time, in short, for a new generation of leadership." Later in the campaign, Kennedy also began to elaborate on the connection between this new generation and its war service: "I think this Nation will rise to the test, and when we do, Mr. Khrushchev will know that a new generation of Americans is taking over this country, a generation that did not fight for world freedom at Anzio or the Solomons in order to see it ripped away."

This was the first of four references in the inaugural to Kennedy's "generation," which was clearly intended to be one of the watchwords of the address. All this talk of a "new generation" and its mission, of course, also evoked FDR's 1936 Democratic National Convention acceptance speech and the declaration that "This generation has a rendezvous with destiny."

Sorensen recalls that Kennedy provided much of the language for this paragraph as the two were trading thoughts in advance of Sorensen's January 16 arrival in Palm Beach. This recollection is supported by the Dictation, in which much of the language first appears. In fact, this paragraph is the place at which the TCS Draft most differs from the succeeding penultimate draft. Five paragraphs of Sorensen's work gave way to one paragraph as the speech was refined. But this was not simply a matter of replacing one approach with another. From the earlier Sorensen draft came the phrases "let the word go forth," "generation of Americans," and "friend or foe."

But the TCS Draft was also filled with pessimistic words and phrases that Kennedy was clearly not willing to adopt.* Among the language proposed by Sorensen and rejected by Kennedy at this juncture was the following:

> And the worst is fast upon us, with the threat of hostile power growing in every corner of our planet. There is not a

---

*Kennedy's insistence on an upbeat tone was specific to the occasion, not to the time period. Nine days later, in his first State of the Union address, he took a very different approach: "Each day the crises multiply. Each day their solution grows more difficult. Each day we grow nearer the hour of maximum danger, as weapons spread and hostile forces grow stronger . . . the tide has been running out and time has not been our friend."

continent, not a country, not a city where the enemies of freedom have not extended their hidden or open assaults.

Yet our alliances in the West are unfulfilled and insecure. Our neighbors to the South are torn by pressures from within and without. Our friends in less-developed states are diverting resources we are loath to replace into useless power struggles.

Meanwhile the grand organization for peace we helped create withers into little more than a forum for invective. The dread secret of the atom we first unlocked spreads slowly, but all too swiftly, around a globe hell-bent for planned or accidental suicide. The instruments of war have far outpaced the instruments of peace.

At this very hour, as we share this ceremony of peaceful change and renewal, there are other voices heard in other lands—some threatening, some despairing, some urging a slow retreat.

Along the way, Kennedy also discarded an allusion to Hamlet—"So let the word go forth to all the world—and *suit the action to the word*" (Hamlet, III, ii, 1)—and a quotation from Patrick Henry he had used at least twice during the campaign about willingness to incur "anguish of spirit . . . , to know the worst and to provide for it."

∽ *Let every nation know, whether it wishes us well or ill, that we shall pay any price, bear any burden, meet any hardship, support any friend, oppose any foe, to assure the survival and the success of liberty.*

Jack Valenti, who wrote speeches for President Lyndon Johnson, has written of this paragraph: "There is imposed here a deliberate rhythm that is the mark of a truly great speech. The rise and fall of the clauses, the immediacy of the moment, the heightening of intensity." Much of that impact, of course, comes from the repeated alliteration: **w**ishes us **w**ell, **p**ay any **p**rice, **b**ear any **b**urden, **f**riend/**f**oe.

Substantively, those who find in the Kennedy inaugural a call to a new imperialism locate it here. But so do those who find in the same speech a timeless call for vigilance against new threats, or for the championing of human rights.

Stylistically, the expression was one toward which Kennedy had been moving. On August 26, 1960, in Detroit he said, "the real question now is whether we are up to the task—whether each and every one of us is willing to face the facts, to bear the burdens." Less than three weeks later in St. Louis he refined the thought: "I don't think that there is any American who would not be willing to bear the burdens and meet his responsibilities if he can insure the freedom of his own country and the success of freedom around the world."

ᔐ *This much we pledge—and more.*

To those old allies whose cultural and spiritual origins we share, we pledge the loyalty of faithful friends. United, there is little we cannot do in a host of cooperative ventures. Divided, there is little we can do—for we dare not meet a powerful challenge at odds and split asunder.

To those new States whom we welcome to the ranks of the free, we pledge our word that one form of colonial control shall not have passed away merely to be replaced by a far more iron tyranny. We shall not always expect to find them supporting our view. But we shall always hope to find them strongly supporting their own freedom—and to remember that, in the past, those who foolishly sought power by riding the back of the tiger ended up inside.

To those people in the huts and villages of half the globe struggling to break the bonds of mass misery, we pledge our best effort to help them help themselves, for whatever period is required—not because the communists may be doing it, not because we seek their votes, but because it is right. If a free society cannot help the many who are poor, it cannot save the few who are rich.

This portion of the speech began a series of messages expressly directed at audiences around the world—Western allies, newly independent former colonies, what we would today call Third World peoples, Latin America, the United Nations, and, finally and most significantly, the Soviet Union. Sorensen says this approach was one Kennedy outlined in one of their first conversations about the address, and the structure is consistent from the earliest surviving draft.

As we have seen, much of the specific language—including the calls to allies to reap the benefits of standing united and to avoid the pitfalls of division, to renounce colonial ambitions, to face down the Soviets in the Third World, and to pledge support for poor countries—comes from Adlai Stevenson's contributions, as improved by Sorensen's editing. It was further sharpened by a Galbraith suggestion on January 18: that "a host of *joint* ventures" become "a host of *cooperative* ventures." The former, Galbraith said, "sounded like a mining partnership."

At the same time, as the speech was being completed, Galbraith also convinced Sorensen to change a number of second-person references to the audiences being addressed, to the third person. Galbraith recalls, "I made a number of suggestions, mostly cosmetic, though I urged the elimination of a mildly hectoring tone toward the allies and the poor countries." Many phrases were changed in these paragraphs and the succeeding one:

BEFORE (Penultimate Draft)	AFTER (JFK reading copy)
We shall not always expect to find *you on our side.*	We shall not always expect to find *them supporting our every view.*

BEFORE (Penultimate Draft)	AFTER (JFK reading copy)
But we shall always expect to find *you vigorously on the side of your own* freedom . . .	But we shall always hope to find *them strongly supporting their own* freedom . . .
To those . . . struggling to break the bonds of mass misery, we pledge our best efforts to *help you help yourselves*, for whatever period is required—not because our enemies are doing it, not because we seek *your* votes, but because it is right.	To those . . . struggling to break the bonds of mass misery, we pledge our best efforts to *help them help themselves*, for whatever period is required—not because the communists are doing it, not because we seek *their* votes, but because it is right.
your peaceful revolution of hope *must not* become the *tool* of hostile powers.	*this* peaceful revolution of hope *cannot* become the *prey* of hostile powers.

As noted above, Stevenson and Galbraith had supplied much of the original basis for the paragraph addressed to the Third World. (Sorensen, reminded that Stevenson contributed what became the sentence, "*If a free society cannot help the many who are poor, it cannot save the few who are rich*," says, "That's a Stevenson line? It's a good line.") Not all of Galbraith's editorial suggestions for this part of the speech were accepted, however.

The line reminding the newly independent nations that "in the past, those who foolishly sought power by riding the back of the tiger ended up inside," which drew the only laughter of the speech from the audience, actually came from a limerick:

There was a young lady of Niger
Who smiled as she rode on a tiger;

They returned from the ride with the lady inside,
And the smile on the face of the tiger.

Galbraith objected. "I thought it out of tune. Others differed." Among those others were Sorensen, and later Kennedy. And Kennedy was not the only statesman to have drawn on the limerick for inspiration. In 1938, after Munich, Winston Churchill told the House of Commons, "Dictators ride to and fro upon tigers which they dare not dismount. And the tigers are getting hungry." Kennedy took note of Churchill's formulation years later:

> Winston Churchill once said that a dictator rides a tiger, he can't get off it and he has to keep it fed. Well, to a lesser degree a politician rides a tiger, too. It isn't that hungry and it isn't that strong, but sometimes it's difficult to tell whether you or the tiger is setting the course.

In making use of this metaphor, Kennedy refined the line considerably on delivery, turning "those who foolishly sought to find power by riding on the tiger's back inevitably ended up inside" to "those who foolishly sought power by riding the back of the tiger ended up inside." The Kennedy version not only shortened the ten-word middle of the sentence to eight words, but also gave it far more punch.

ᗌ *To our sister republics south of our border, we offer a special pledge— to convert our good words into good deeds—in a new alliance for progress—to assist free men and free governments in casting off the chains of poverty. But this peaceful revolution of hope cannot become the prey of hostile powers. Let all our neighbors know that we shall join with them to oppose aggression or subversion anywhere in the Americas. And let every other power know that this Hemisphere intends to remain the master of its own house.*

The inaugural address was actually the first time John Kennedy had uttered the phrase "alliance for progress" in a speech—but not for Sorensen's lack of trying to get him to do so.

During the campaign, Kennedy had solicited suggestions for a "policy label" for a new Latin American initiative. Sorensen responded with "*alianza*," "assuming that it had a broader meaning than 'alliance' because it was the name of an insurance cooperative organized by some of our Mexican-American supporters," and, he now confesses, because "to me [the word] had such a musical ring." Ernesto Betancourt, a Latin American expert in Washington, conveyed through Sorensen aide Richard Goodwin the addition of "*para el progreso*" "although," Sorensen notes, "for some time we mistakenly dropped the '*el.*'

The phrase—without the "*el*"—was included in the prepared text of Kennedy's October 18, 1960, speech on Latin American policy in Tampa, Florida, and disseminated to the reporters covering it, but Kennedy dropped it on delivery. Seventeen days later, on November 4 in Chicago, the same phrase again appeared in the advance release text of Kennedy's speech. Sorensen says he may have "tried to put it back in since [Kennedy] hadn't used it" in Tampa. But again Kennedy omitted the language on delivery.

Sorensen's *Kennedy* says that the words "in a new alliance for progress" were added to the inaugural address by Kennedy himself, and only after his return from Palm Beach to Washington on January 17. And indeed, the TCS Draft of this paragraph is nearly identical to the final speech—without this key phrase. But the addition was made by the time of the penultimate draft, that is, either in Palm Beach or on board the *Caroline* on

January 17. Perhaps Kennedy, who had originally sought a new "policy label," thought the inaugural finally the place to use it. Evidence that the choice was Kennedy's can be found in the use of only the English version of the phrase; the new president was uncomfortable with foreign languages, perhaps accounting for his earlier dropping of the label from his campaign addresses, where the drafts had called for him to use it in both English and Spanish.

In any event, the impact was considerable. Following his return from a trip to Costa Rica in March 1963, Kennedy told Ben Bradlee that he thought his inaugural address had "meant more to Latin Americans than to anyone else."

 To that world assembly of sovereign states, the United Nations, our last best hope in an age where the instruments of war have far outpaced the instruments of peace, we renew our pledge of support—to prevent it from becoming merely a forum for invective—to strengthen its shield of the new and the weak—and to enlarge the area in which its writ may run.

Kennedy's reference to the United Nations as "our last best hope" resonated with centuries of presidential rhetoric as well as months of his own.

In his first inaugural address, in 1801, Thomas Jefferson had referred to "this Government, the world's best hope." Echoing Jefferson in even more memorable words in his annual message to Congress for 1862—the written precursor to the modern State of the Union address—Abraham Lincoln had written, "We shall nobly save, or meanly lose, the last best hope of earth." Kennedy shared the sentiment, telling a Boston audience in 1954, "We are in truth the last best hope on earth."

Sorensen says that Lincoln was the source for Kennedy's phrasing with respect to the UN. But tying Lincoln's words to the world organization actually seems to have begun with Dwight Eisenhower. In his second inaugural address, in 1957, Eisenhower had also reaffirmed a pledge "to honor, and to strive to fortify, the authority of the United Nations. For in that body rests the best hope of our age for the assertion of that law by which all nations may live in dignity." Candidate Kennedy picked up on this theme in his September 14, 1960, campaign address to a group of Democratic women in New York, where Nikita Khrushchev was in the middle of his twenty-five-day visit. Kennedy said,

> We have been successful in limiting Mr. Khrushchev to New York, but we have not been successful in limiting his influence in Africa, Asia, and Latin America. At its best or at its worst, the United Nations remains a symbol of all that we hope, of all that we believe, of all that we look forward to.

Later in the same speech Kennedy referred to the UN as "the last great hope of peace." In 1960–1961 support for the United Nations had not yet become a matter of partisan or ideological dispute in the mainstream of American politics.

Sorensen has acknowledged, however, that Kennedy

> spoke in many overlapping and conflicting roles: as the champion of the Free World and a seeker of one world, as a believer in the United Nations and a leader of NATO, SEATO, and the OAS. The United States, he knew, could not achieve its goals relying only on the force of its example, although that needed strengthening, or only on the force of its arms, although they needed strengthening, or only on the United

Nations, which also needed strengthening. There was no single or certain answer.

The contrast between this aspiration and the condemnation of the United Nations as a "forum for invective" was Kennedy's own. Sorensen believes that the phrase "forum for invective" was used to attack the UN in the 1950s, but no such reference could be located. The TCS Draft, it will be recalled, had nearly adopted the phrase "the grand organization for peace we helped create has withered into little more than a forum for invective." Kennedy, however, wished to challenge rather than accept that view.

    Finally, to those nations who would make themselves our adversary, we offer not a pledge but a request: that both sides begin anew the quest for peace, before the dark powers of destruction unleashed by science engulf all humanity in planned or accidental self-destruction.

When, many years later, Sorensen had this paragraph read to him, the feature he picked out was the rhyme of the words "request" and "quest." This was an example, he said, of "my hobby of writing, mostly for family audiences, doggerel [that] often influenced speeches: let every nation *know* / friend and *foe* alike [or] *request* / join us in a *quest*." The first of these two examples is even more obvious as a rhyme in the earlier TCS Draft: "let every nation know, be it friend or foe."

Nor is this evolution quite as unusual as it may at first appear. As Garry Wills observed in *Lincoln at Gettysburg,*

Lincoln, like most writers of great prose, began by writing bad poetry. Early experiments with words are almost always stilted, formal, tentative. Economy of words, grip, precision come later (if at all).

If a habit of Sorensen's gave rise to one part of this paragraph, another was pure Kennedy. The TCS Draft referred to the "dark powers of destruction" "engulf[ing] us all in ruin." But the final speech spoke instead, more specifically, of "planned or accidental self-destruction." This was a reflection of Kennedy's fixation on the risk that nuclear war could result from miscalculation:

> . . . the fear that one side or both sides might miscalculate the other side's vital interests, and likely response, and the power available to them. . . . The word "accidental" [in the inaugural] did not refer to mechanical error, or technical error, a bomb causing to go off or a rocket to be launched by mistake, it referred to human error, where a mistake would be the last ever made.

ᔐ *We dare not tempt them with weakness. For only when our arms are sufficient beyond doubt can we be certain beyond doubt that they will never be employed.*

These two crisp sentences summed up much of what John Kennedy had learned from the Second World War—the formative experience of his political life and of his generation—and much of how he intended to apply that learning to his presidency.

It is particularly remarkable, then, that the first sentence—"*We dare not tempt them with weakness*"—comes word for word from the draft inaugural submitted by Adlai Stevenson, a man Kennedy thought fatally weak. In fact, Sorensen had taken Stevenson's sentence and changed one word—"dare not tempt *them*" became "dare not tempt *you*" in the TCS Draft—only to have the word changed back during the seventy-two hours before the speech was delivered, as part of the effort to soften the address by removing most of the first- and second-person references.

Sorensen has said that the second sentence—"*only when our arms are sufficient beyond doubt can we be certain beyond doubt*"— "tells us more about John F. Kennedy's foreign policy in the years that followed than the more famous 'Ask not.'" In fact, he says, it is "the most important sentence in the speech."

The thought was not a new one for Kennedy. In the 1940 senior thesis at Harvard that later became *Why England Slept*, Kennedy had written, "We must always keep our armaments equal to our commitments." In the 1960 campaign, at St. Louis on October 2, Kennedy had quoted Churchill's 1946 "iron curtain" speech in Fulton, Missouri, when Churchill had said of the Soviets that "there is nothing they so much admire as strength, and there is nothing for which they have less respect than weakness." On September 16, 1960, at Seattle, Kennedy himself had observed, "We can convince Mr. Khrushchev to bargain seriously for peace only when our strength makes clear to him that no war will ever be to his advantage. . . . The only way we can get his agreement to disarmament is by our strength of armaments, enough to stop the next war before it starts." Or, as Arthur Schlesinger had written during the campaign, "we will arm to disarm."

∽ *But neither can two great and powerful groups of nations take comfort from our present course—both sides overburdened by the cost of modern weapons, both rightly alarmed by the steady spread of the deadly atom, both racing to alter that uncertain balance of terror that stays the hand of mankind's final war.*

The opening portion of this passage is one of the few for which the first draft of the speech survives. It contained two important differences from the final version: referring to "two great and powerful nations" rather than "two great and powerful *groups of nations*," and to "this *reckless* course" rather than "our present course." Both changes came only in the final editing on January 17–18; both considerably soften the passage.

The phrase "balance of terror," familiar now, was of recent vintage in 1961. Its origins can be traced to an article, "The Delicate Balance of Terror," by the strategist Albert Wohlstetter, published in the closing weeks of 1958. As its title indicates, Wohlstetter was focused on the delicacy of the balance, which he called "in fact precarious." Much of Wohlstetter's analysis dealt with the optimal mix and deployment of nuclear forces, but his argument also offered strong support to Maxwell Taylor's doctrine of "flexible response," and particularly the need for an increase in U.S. conventional forces. Wohlstetter, a senior policy analyst at the Rand Corporation, also expressed significant concern about accidental nuclear war, or war as a result of miscalculation. On all these scores, "The Delicate Balance of Terror" no doubt found an attentive reader in Senator John Kennedy.

✍ *So let us begin anew—remembering on both sides that civility is not a sign of weakness, and sincerity is always subject to proof. Let us never negotiate out of fear. But let us never fear to negotiate.*

While the phrases "negotiate out of fear" / "fear to negotiate" came from the Galbraith drafts,* it is worth noting as well that, in

---

*The acknowledgment that this phrase had been originally crafted by Galbraith was apparently the earliest indication that anyone other than Kennedy had written any important part of the inaugural address. This fact was first published no later than 1964. During his lifetime, Kennedy clearly sought to limit such claims to authorship. When Galbraith, just after the speech, was caught on film discussing "fear to negotiate" with John and Elaine Steinbeck, the new president spanked him: "I've lived in this city about twenty years and have witnessed every kind of self-advertisement you can imagine. But picking out that phrase and then getting Steinbeck to ask about it is beyond anything I've seen."

this one respect at least, Galbraith may—perhaps unconsciously—have been drawing on the Kennedy style. In a National Press Club speech at the outset of his presidential campaign, for instance, Kennedy had declared, "Let us discuss the issues the next President will face—but let us also discuss the powers and tools with which we must face them." On the other hand, the substance—never fearing to negotiate—was not a view Kennedy had always espoused. In a June 1960 Senate speech summing up his approach to foreign and defense policy, and playing off the failure of Eisenhower's Paris meeting with Khrushchev after the Soviets had downed a U-2 spy plane, Kennedy had insisted that a U.S. arms buildup must precede any future summit with the Soviets, "for no President of the United States must ever again be put in the position of traveling across the seas, armed only with vague, speculative hopes, in order to provide an occasion for public humiliation."

The substance of Galbraith's point was hardly novel, however. Throughout the campaign, Kennedy had repeatedly quoted Winston Churchill's similar dictum that "we arm to parley." Sorensen later wrote that this was Kennedy's favorite Churchill quote. And Galbraith included "we arm to parley" itself in both his inaugural drafts.

The sentiment that "civility is not a sign of weakness," on the other hand, was rooted in a particular criticism Kennedy and Sorensen had of an Eisenhower administration gesture: the "foolish" refusal of Secretary of State John Foster Dulles to shake the hand of Chinese envoy Zhou Enlai at negotiations in Geneva in 1954 over the war in Indochina.

✌ *Let both sides explore what problems unite us instead of belaboring those problems which divide us.*

Let both sides, for the first time, formulate serious and precise proposals for the inspection and control of arms—and bring the absolute power to destroy other nations under the absolute control of all nations.

Let both sides seek to invoke the wonders of science instead of its terrors. Together let us explore the stars, conquer the deserts, eradicate disease, tap the ocean depths, and encourage the arts and commerce.

Much of the language on potential areas of cooperation with the Soviets came from Stevenson, but this was not a new thought for Kennedy. In his 1956 commencement address at Harvard University, Kennedy had said, "Let us not emphasize all on which we differ but all we have in common. Let us consider not what we fear separately but what we share together."

Let both sides unite to heed in all corners of the earth the command of Isaiah—to "undo the heavy burdens . . . (and) let the oppressed go free."

This is the first of the two biblical quotations in the speech, and the only one from the Old Testament. It comes from chapter 58, verse 6 of Isaiah:

Is not this the fast I have chosen?
To loose the fetters of wickedness,
To undo the heavy burdens,
And to let the oppressed go free,
And that ye break every yoke?

Sorensen says that this quotation was suggested to him by Rabbi Issac Franck of the Washington, D.C., Jewish Council, from whom he occasionally solicited Old Testament references. The passage was included, in its abbreviated form, in the TCS Draft. In the penultimate draft, Kennedy and Sorensen expanded the reference to take in some of verses 7 and 8 as well. The full passage continues:

Is it not to deal thy bread to the hungry,
And that thou bring the poor that are cast out into thy house?

When thou seest the naked, that thou cover him, and that
thou hide not thyself from thine own flesh?

Then shall thy light break forth as the morning,
And thy healing shall spring forth speedily;
And thy righteousness shall go before thee,
The glory of the Lord shall be thy rearward.

The penultimate draft proposed to condense all of this to: "loose
the fetters of wickedness . . . undo the heavy burdens . . . let the
oppressed go free . . . deal thy bread to the hungry . . . bring the
poor into thy house . . . (For) then shall thy light break forth as
the morning. . . . " But, Sorensen now says, "the whole thing,
while excellent, was too long. This got the message across." The
final text reverted to the abbreviated quotation advanced in the
TCS Draft.

Biblical quotations were, of course, not new to presidential
inaugurals. While nearly every president, beginning with Washington, had invoked God, John Quincy Adams had been the first
to cite scripture in his speech when he quoted Psalm 127 that "except the Lord keep the city the watchman waketh but in vain."
Lincoln, while the fourteenth president to deliver an inaugural
address, was only the second to invoke biblical language when he
quoted or paraphrased four passages in his second inaugural.

Like Lincoln, Kennedy used the Bible not to invoke divine
blessing but to help establish the tone of the address as a whole.
Henry Fairlie refers to Kennedy's

> belief that there is a source of energy in a society which is
> greater than its parts, that the people may be exhorted to
> transcend, not only the limits of their politics, but their own
> limitations. This is a religious belief, and the inspiration of the
> inaugural address was religious.

Indeed, as Fairlie points out, the scriptural language in the address was not confined to the actual biblical quotations but also drew on reiteration with "the power of liturgy," what students of rhetoric call anaphora, the use of similar words to begin successive statements: *Let every nation know . . . , Let all our neighbors know . . . , let every other power know . . . , let us begin anew . . . , Let us never negotiate out of fear. But let us never fear to negotiate. Let both sides explore . . . , Let both sides, for the first time, formulate serious and precise proposals . . . , Let both sides seek to invoke . . . , Together let us explore . . . , Let both sides unite . . . , let both sides join . . . , let us begin.* This "repeated and elegantly phrased invitation to mutual pledge-making" "is essential to the rite of investiture" that is at the heart of inaugurals.

ᔕ *And if a beachhead of cooperation may push back the jungle of suspicion, let both sides join in creating a new endeavor, not a new balance of power, but a new world of law, where the strong are just and the weak secure and the peace preserved.*

All this will not be finished in the first 100 days. Nor will it be finished in the first 1,000 days, nor in the life of this Administration, nor even perhaps in our lifetime on this planet. But let us begin.

One subject on which John Kennedy's thinking seems to have changed somewhat during his transition to the presidency was the extent to which he wished to emulate Franklin Roosevelt's whirlwind initial period in office, the immortal "Hundred Days."

On October 12, 1960, campaigning in New York City, Kennedy had said,

If there is anything that history has taught us, it is that the great accomplishments of Woodrow Wilson and of Franklin Roosevelt were made in the early days, months, and years of their administrations. That was the time for maximum action. . . . Now is the time to prepare for what we must do in the winter of 1961. . . . October is the month to prepare for action in January, February, and March.

But the scholar and former Truman aide Richard Neustadt, whose recent book *Presidential Power: The Politics of Leadership* Kennedy had read and admired, warned otherwise. Asked for a memorandum on "Organizing the Transition," Neustadt began by warning against "The Problem of Another 'Hundred Days.'" Kennedy was likely to lack Roosevelt's advantage of large congressional majorities and an air of crisis demanding strong leadership. Expectations were too high, Neustadt warned, and every interest in Washington was inclined to see its priorities as those of a prospective Kennedy administration. "These legislative wants are hard to square with a convincing demonstration of energy and accomplishment. 'Another Hundred Days' as an impression of effectiveness is threatened by the promissory notes read into that analogy."

Within weeks, Kennedy seemed to take this advice to heart and began to back away from the very expectations he had been working to build. On October 23 in Madison, Wisconsin, instead of talking about Wilson and Roosevelt's first months and his own first weeks, Kennedy was taking a somewhat longer view:

. . . unless the next President of the United States is prepared for action when he gets elected, then he will lose January, February, March, April, and May of 1961, which should be his best and most vigorous months.

Woodrow Wilson and Franklin Roosevelt made their greatest contribution to the advancement of this country in their first 2 years. . . .

By the time he had actually been elected, Sorensen found Kennedy "irritated . . . by widespread press speculation that he intended to emulate the first hundred days of Franklin Roosevelt."

Galbraith addressed this concern in the draft inaugural he presented to Kennedy on December 23 in Palm Beach, and refined the thought in the second draft he offered on January 9 in Cambridge. Sorensen then worked the words further for the TCS draft:

GALBRAITH 1	GALBRAITH 2	SORENSEN
And the tasks of which I speak today will not soon be finished. The work of this Administration will not be over in a hundred days, or in five hundred days or in a thousand days. Its labors will continue, without remission, for all of the next four years	The tasks of which I speak today will not be finished. And the work of this new Administration will not be over in a hundred days, or in five hundred days, or in a thousand days. Its work will continue without surcease for all of the next four years.	All this will not be finished in the first one hundred days. Nor will it be finished in the first one thousand days, nor in the life of this Administration, nor even perhaps in our life-time on this planet. But let us begin. . . .

The phrase "a thousand days" evoked Winston Churchill's admonition to the House of Commons in June 1940: "Let us therefore brace ourselves to our duties, and so bear ourselves that, if the British Empire and its Commonwealth last for a thousand years, men will still say, 'This was their finest hour.'"

One possibly ironic footnote to history: *A Thousand Days* became the title of Athur Schlesinger's prizewinning account of the Kennedy administration. As Galbraith acknowledged at the time, Schlesinger contributed to at least one of the drafts he gave Kennedy. Was Schlesinger himself the author of the phrase "a thousand days"? Schlesinger does not recall. Galbraith also has "no specific memory" on this, but says, "My recollection and also the sense of style would lead me to believe that the reference to 'a thousand days' was Professor Schlesinger's."

Galbraith has written that he suggested the words "Let us begin" on January 17 as a conclusion to this passage, "to give proper cadence, and a day or two later it was mildly historic." In fact, as the comparison above indicates, it was Sorensen who identified the cadence. But the story of the origins of this particular phrase is even more complicated: its first appearance comes in Galbraith's first draft of the inaugural, in which the speech as a whole (not this passage) ends with the words, "Let us begin." Galbraith dropped this from his second draft, but presumably not before Sorensen had picked it up and relocated it.

ᔢ *In your hands, my fellow citizens, more than mine, will rest the final success or failure of our course. Since this country was founded, each generation of Americans has been summoned to give testimony to its national loyalty. The graves of young Americans who answered the call to service surround the globe.*

The opening phrases of this passage came directly from Lincoln's first inaugural. Lincoln had begun his concluding thought about the possibility of secession by declaring, "In *your* hands, my dissatisfied fellow-countrymen, and not in *mine*, is the momentous issue of civil war" (emphasis in original). But while Lincoln sought to dissuade action, Kennedy was just beginning his most important call to action.

Yet Kennedy insisted that the call be one based on optimism, not fear. The TCS Draft is very different from the final address at this point. It conjures up a nightmare vision:

> Were we to suffer open armed attack, our decision would be clear, our response instant, our dedication to the cause complete. We would not pause to count the cost or weigh the odds. We would not heed the voices of surrender, fear or panic. Every man and every woman would answer the call of the trumpet.

But Kennedy sought to inspire service out of dedication and loyalty rather than fear. He would find inspiration in the example of the dead of recent wars—including his own elder brother—but not in an appeal to service based on anxiety. He first framed the wording in his dictation of January 10: "Since this country was founded, every generation of Americans has been called at least once to give testimony to their national loyalty. The graves of young Americans who responded circles [sic] the globe."

In the manuscript for *Kennedy*, though not in the published version, Sorensen quoted a later version of this paragraph, "a passage [Kennedy] dictated as we discussed ideas":

> This heritage has been passed to us by other Americans who in every generation since our nation began have answered the call to service. Many lie buried around the globe. Now in 1961 we face another call to the defense of freedom. It may not require us to give our lives, but it will require us to . . .

∽ Now the trumpet summons us again—not as a call to bear arms, though arms we need; not as a call to battle, though embattled we are— but a call to bear the burden of a long twilight struggle, year in and year

out, "rejoicing in hope, patient in tribulation"—a struggle against the common enemies of man: tyranny, poverty, disease, and war itself.

Can we forge against these enemies a grand and global alliance, North and South, East and West, that can assure a more fruitful life for all mankind? Will you join in that historic effort?

The image of the trumpet calling the people to service is of uncertain origin. In Act V, Scene 2 of Shakespeare's *King John,* Lewis asks, "What lusty trumpet doth summon us?"* But quite possibly the image in the minds of Kennedy and Sorensen was at once both more ancient and more modern than that. Maxwell Taylor, as we have seen, had written a book just a year or so earlier that had played a significant role in shaping Kennedy's strategic military thinking. Taylor had called the book *The Uncertain Trumpet,* and the quotation at the outset of the book made clear his reference to First Corinthians 14:8. It is there written, "For if the trumpet give an uncertain sound, who shall prepare himself to the battle?" Kennedy had alluded to this quotation repeatedly in campaign speeches.

---

*The *New York Times*, on the day after the inaugural, purported to find an antecedent in another Shakespeare passage. Citing no source and offering no byline, the *Times* declared that "In President Kennedy's peroration today, his trumpet call to the struggle against the 'common enemies of man,' many here today heard an echo of King Henry V's challenge to his troops before Agincourt . . . :

> From this day to the ending of the world,
> But we in it shall be remembered:
> And gentlemen in England now a-bed
> Shall think themselves accursed they were not here,
> And hold their manhoods cheap whiles any speaks
> That fought with us upon Saint Crispin's Day."

There is no question that this passage from *King Henry V* was one of Kennedy's favorites. It is not at all clear what the passage has to do with this section of the inaugural address.

The inaugural passage itself is one on which we may have the clearest indication of the way the Kennedy-Sorensen collaboration worked in practice. The TCS Draft contains an early version of this "trumpet" paragraph. But Sorensen's file also contains a revised version, in Sorensen's own hand, corresponding precisely with the penultimate draft (and the final speech as delivered). The handwritten fragment was scribbled by Sorensen on the back of a telegram from U.S. Senator Ernest Gruening, delivered at 6:31 P.M. on January 11, which Sorensen presumably found on his desk or in his briefcase and used as scratch paper. Sorensen agrees that this is likely the reason he wrote on the back of the telegram. It seems quite likely that it reflected language crafted by Sorensen and Kennedy during a conversation, possibly the call Sorensen recalls at the Goldberg brunch on January 15 or while the men worked at poolside in Palm Beach on the 16th and 17th. A comparison of the TCS Draft, Kennedy's dictation of January 10, and the Gruening telegram fragment illustrates how the passage evolved; words in brackets in the Gruening telegram version were scratched through, as if the passage was crafted and edited at one sitting:

TCS DRAFT	KENNEDY DICTATION	GRUENING TELEGRAM FRAGMENT
Today the trumpet sounds its urgent call again—not a call to arms, though arms we need—not a call to battle though embattled we	Today we sound the trumpet once again, not as a call to arms, though arms we need, not as a call to battle though embattled we are,	Now the trumpet summons us again— not as a call to arms, though arms we need—not as a call to battle, though embattled we are—

are—but a call to
a broader, more basic
struggle against
all the enemies of
man—tyranny and
poverty and war
itself.

rather a call for a
broader, deeper
struggle against the
common enemies
of man: tyranny,
poverty, disease
and war itself.

but a call [to meet
and endure] to bear
the burden of
a long twilight
struggle, year
in and year out,
"rejoicing in
hope, patient in
tribulation"—
a [burden] struggle
against the common
enemies of man:
tyranny, poverty,
disease and war
itself.

Some of this language bears a striking resemblance to a phrase in President Eisenhower's farewell address to the nation, the speech best known for its warning of a "military–industrial complex." Eisenhower had referred to "the burdens of a prolonged and complex struggle" while Kennedy spoke of "the burden of a long twilight struggle." But, unlikely as it seems, this must apparently be chalked up to coincidence. Eisenhower's speech was closely held until delivered on the evening of January 17, while the penultimate draft of the inaugural was completed before Kennedy arrived in Washington earlier that same day.

At the same time the second biblical quotation, this one from the New Testament, was added to the speech. The words came from Romans 12:

Be kindly affectioned one to another with brotherly love; in honor preferring one another;

> Not slothful in business; fervent in spirit; serving the Lord;
> *Rejoicing in hope; patient in tribulation*; continuing instant in
> prayer;
> Distributing to the necessity of saints; given to hospitality.

Kennedy likely got the quotation from the Reverend Billy Graham, perhaps when the two men played golf on January 16; Sorensen's *Kennedy* says that Kennedy "obtained a list of possible Biblical quotations" from Graham, who presumably would have drawn largely from the New Testament, while Sorensen's source, Rabbi Issac Franck, promoted the Old Testament. Hugh Sidey later reported that Graham had given the president-elect "some twenty-five passages from the Bible" "typed neatly" on "a piece of yellow paper."

✎ *In the long history of the world, only a few generations have been granted the role of defending freedom in its hour of maximum danger. I do not shrink from this responsibility—I welcome it. I do not believe that any of us would exchange places with any other people or any other generation. The energy, the faith, the devotion which we bring to this endeavor will light our country and all who serve it—and the glow from that fire can truly light the world.*

The idea that freedom was living through its "hour of maximum danger" was one that had marked Kennedy's campaign for the presidency from its beginning. In declaring for the Democratic nomination on the second day of 1960, Kennedy said that he had "developed an image of America as fulfilling a noble and historic role as the defender of freedom in a time of maximum peril."

The particular language of this paragraph of the inaugural address came almost entirely from the Kennedy dictation of

January 10. This passage was the most extensive drawn from the dictation.

The fire image is one of Kennedy's most enduring; it probably inspired the eternal flame that marks his grave. But, as noted, it actually drew on the first inaugural address ever delivered by an American president, Washington's declaration that "the sacred fire of liberty . . . [had been] entrusted to the hands of the American people." And Washington likely drew on Thomas Paine, who wrote that "From a small spark kindled in America, a flame has arisen not to be extinguished."*

∽ *And so, my fellow Americans: ask not what your country can do for you—ask what you can do for your country.*

These are unquestionably the best-remembered words in Kennedy's speech, and their origins have been the object of much speculation.

Bartlett's Familiar Quotations cites four antecedents:

- An 1884 Memorial Day address by Oliver Wendell Holmes, Jr., to a group of fellow Civil War veterans, in which the future Supreme Court justice said, "For stripped of the temporary associations which gave rise to it, it is now the moment when by common consent we pause to

---

*In the penultimate draft of the address, this paragraph ended with a third biblical quotation—"For 'when a man's ways please the Lord, he maketh even his enemies to be at peace with him'"—from Proverbs 16:7. This was apparently one of the offerings Kennedy had received from Billy Graham. Sorensen's *Kennedy* says this quotation was removed in-flight on January 17, but Kennedy pointed it out during the flight to Hugh Sidey and it appears in the penultimate draft, meaning that it was removed only after Kennedy and Sorensen's return to Washington. The quotation was later included in Kennedy's 1963 speech at American University.

become conscious of our national life and to rejoice in it, to recall what our country had done for each of us, and to ask ourselves what we can do for our country in return."

- An essay in a 1904 book by Le Baron Russell Briggs, a Harvard English professor, in which he wrote, "As has often been said, the youth who loves his Alma Mater will always ask, not 'What can she do for me?' but 'What can I do for her?'"

- A speech by Senator (and future President) Warren Harding to the 1916 Republican National Convention asserting that "In the great fulfillment we must have a citizenship less concerned about what the government can do for it and more anxious about what it can do for the nation."

- Arthur Schlesinger, Jr.'s statement in *A Thousand Days* that "This thought had lain in Kennedy's mind for a long time," and remarking on Kennedy's entry in a notebook in 1945 of a quotation from Rousseau, "As soon as any man says of the affairs of the state, What does it matter to me? the state may be given up as lost."

And there is more. Schlesinger also quoted a eulogy contained in the writing of Van Wyck Brooks: "Here we may be reminded that man is most honored, not by that which a city may do for him, but by that which he has done for the city." And the thought had apparently also long lain in the mind of Harding. In his own inaugural address, Harding said, "Our most dangerous tendency is to expect too much of government, and at the same time do for it too little." Sorensen acknowledges that he read Harding's inaugural but denies that Harding was the source for Kennedy's statement.

Two other oft-cited sources for "ask not" can also be dismissed. Some published accounts credit Kahlil Gibran because a sentence in an article by Gibran written in Arabic sometime between 1920 and 1923 has been translated as "Are you a politician asking what your country can do for you, or a zealous one asking what you can do for your country." But Professor Suheil Bushrui, director of the Kahlil Gibran Research and Studies Project at the University of Maryland's Center for International Development and Conflict Management, points out that this English translation of the Gibran passage was not published until 1965, and that a literal translation of the same passage would be "Are you a politician who says to himself, 'I want to derive benefit from my nation [country]'; or an enthusiastic and earnestly concerned one who whispers to himself, 'I desire to benefit my nation [country].'"

Others have suggested that Kennedy borrowed the phrase from Dr. George St. John, the headmaster of Choate, the boarding school Kennedy attended, who is supposed to have asked, referring to the landscape surrounding the school, "Ask not what the hills can do for you, but what you can do for the hills." But Choate's archivist, the author of the school's official history, and St. John's son Seymour, who succeeded him as headmaster, "all consider it wishful thinking at best."

Kennedy and Sorensen had been working toward the thought summed up by "ask not" throughout the 1960 campaign:

- In an early campaign speech at the National Press Club, on January 14, 1960, Kennedy said, "We will need in the sixties a President who is willing and able to summon his national constituency to its finest hour . . . to demand of them the sacrifices that will be necessary."
- In his acceptance speech in July at the Democratic National Convention, he said, "The New Frontier of which I speak is not a set of promises—it is a set of challenges. It sums up not what I intend to offer the American people, but what I intend to ask of them."

- On the campaign trail in Anchorage, Alaska, on September 3 he referred to "a state of mind. Those people in this country who do not want things done for them, but want to do them themselves."
- Two days later in Detroit, Kennedy was crisper: "The New Frontier is not what I promise I am going to do for you. The New Frontier is what I ask you to do for our country."
- On September 20, in Washington, D.C., he said, "We do not campaign stressing what our country is going to do for us as a people. We stress what we can do for the country, all of us."

The peroration of the earliest TCS Draft of the inaugural began, "So ask not what your country is going to do for you. Ask what you can do for your country." In his January 10 dictation, Kennedy made this, "*My fellow Americans*: ask not what your country *will* do for you, ask rather what you can do for your country." By the penultimate draft, this had become, "And so, my fellow Americans: ask not what your country will do for you— ask what you can do for your country." That is the form in which the sentence appeared in Kennedy's reading copy. Only on delivery did Kennedy change it from "what your country *will* do for you" to the more parallel—and powerful—"what your country *can* do for you."

How the campaign versions morphed into the phrasing in the early drafts of the inaugural remains something of a mystery. The account in Sorensen's *Kennedy* that the president-elect "worked and re-worked" the sentence in Palm Beach on the morning of January 17 with the Anchorage, Detroit, and Washington speeches "spread out . . . beside him" is incorrect. But all that Sorensen will offer is this:

. . . for decades my standard answer to the oft-repeated question, Who came up with the words "ask not what your country can do for you"? etc.—I usually say to people, "I have answered that question 1416 times, yours is the 1,417th, so I will give you the same answer," and they say, "What's that?" and I say, "Ask not."

The influence of Strunk is once again apparent. Stunk's Rule 11 is "Put statements in positive form." He warns of "the weakness inherent in the word *not*," and therefore favors "dishonest" to "not honest" and "trifling" to "not important." At the same time, however, Strunk notes that "The antithesis of negative and positive is strong: Not charity, but simple justice. Not that I loved Caesar less, but that I loved Rome more." This power of antithesis lies at the heart of the climax of Kennedy's speech: ask *not* . . . , ask. . . . The thought itself is not original, but the Kennedy-Sorensen formulation is. And that is why Warren Harding's words are not remembered while John Kennedy's cannot be forgotten.

ᴖ *My fellow citizens of the world: ask not what America will do for you, but what together we can do for the freedom of man.*

Finally, whether you are citizens of America or citizens of the world, ask of us here the same high standards of strength and sacrifice which we ask of you.

Following the first "ask not," directed to the American people, with a second addressed to "fellow citizens of the world" was one of the contributions made by Kennedy's dictation of January 10. It hearkened back to Franklin Roosevelt's last, abbreviated inaugural address, in which he said, "We have learned to be citizens of the world." And it drew on a point Kennedy himself had made repeatedly during the 1960 campaign. Noting that

Thomas Paine had written that "The cause of America is the cause of all mankind," Kennedy turned this around to say that "in 1960, the cause of all mankind is the cause of America." As noted, the final wording of the sentence was suggested on January 17 or 18 by Dean Rusk.

✍ *With a good conscience our only sure reward, with history the final judge of our deeds, let us go forth to lead the land we love, asking His blessing and His help, but knowing that here on earth God's work must truly be our own.*

An address that had begun with a reference to God thus ended with one as well. Nor was this unusual or unexpected. Every one of the twenty-nine men who had earlier given inaugural addresses, save Theodore Roosevelt, had also concluded at least one of their inaugural addresses with a word about God.*

With the exception of only three later word changes, Kennedy's conclusion was included in the TCS Draft found in the president's files. Moreover, unlike the rest of that draft, which was typed, these final words were added to the draft in Sorensen's handwriting, perhaps as a last addition before giving the draft to Kennedy.

---

*The only six of the forty-three inaugural addresses before Kennedy's not to end with some reference to God are Washington's abbreviated second, Madison's second, Grant's second, McKinley's second, TR's and Wilson's second. President Eisenhower had taken the role of God in inaugural addresses to new lengths, beginning his first with what he called "a private prayer," and both beginning and concluding his second with prayers of the sort beginning "May we . . ."

Lyndon Johnson and Jimmy Carter, like TR, did not invoke God as they closed. But more recently, the conclusion to inaugural addresses has become even more formulaic. The last seven inaugural addresses, beginning with Ronald Reagan in 1981, have closed with the words "God bless America" or a minor variant of that phrase.

The wording had been drawn from the Massachusetts Legislature speech of January 9, which Kennedy had concluded as follows: "Humbly I ask his help in this undertaking—but aware that on earth His will is worked by men, I ask your help and your prayers, as I embark on this new and solemn journey." The decision to make the same point again may have been reinforced by the conclusion of the draft Louis Harris submitted to Kennedy on Saturday, January 14: "We ask for divine guidance in a terrible hour of crisis between the quick and the dead. But let their [sic] be no doubt about it, our own salvation lies in what we do—you and I together—in the turning point days ahead."

Working with a draft in Palm Beach a couple of days later, Kennedy told Sorensen that the inaugural "sounds an awful lot like" the previous week's Massachusetts speech. "Yes," Sorensen acknowledged, "but I changed it a bit." Kennedy responded, "I guess it's OK."

Two word changes were made in Palm Beach, however. A "*clear* conscience" became a "*good*" one, and history became the final judge of "our *deeds*" rather than of "our *motives*." One word was added sometime on January 17 or 18: Kennedy invoked "His blessing and *His* help" rather than just "His blessing and help."

But overall Sorensen seems to have overcome Galbraith's reluctance to "write another's prayers." The product of a father who had abandoned fundamentalist Christianity, and a Jewish mother, Sorensen acknowledges that while he did not discuss the theology of the conclusion with Kennedy, "it is consistent with the beliefs of the Unitarian Church in which I was raised." Nor did this go completely unnoticed. William Lee Miller, who grew up with Sorensen, later noted that this passage "reflected a humanism at least as compatible with the speechwriter's formal religious background as with that of [Kennedy]."

Robert Bellah, without the benefit of Sorensen's observation (and without making the connection to Sorensen's involvement or upbringing), had noted this more than thirty-five years earlier when he termed the God of America's "civil religion," of which he found Kennedy's inaugural evocative, "rather 'unitarian.'" Bellah declared, "The whole address can be understood as only the most recent statement of a theme that lies very deep in the American tradition, namely the obligation, both collective and individual, to carry out God's will on earth."

Part Three

After

A t Gettysburg, Lincoln had said that his words would be "little note[d], nor long remembere[d]," and at first that seemed to be the case, as press accounts were minimal and popular reaction muted. But Lincoln's speech was not broadcast live on national television, and for John Kennedy's inaugural address the response was immediate and dramatic.

The front page of the next day's *Washington Post* called the speech "surely one of the most eloquent in history." The *New York Times* editorial spoke of "the eloquent words of a superb inaugural address distinguished for its style and brevity as well as for its meaty content." Even Republican papers joined in the applause. The *New York Herald Tribune* thought "The speech was compact, the words were moving and the sentiments were those which all men of goodwill can share." The *Los Angeles Times* said Kennedy had gotten off to "about as good a start as a president of the United States could make."

Across the nation, writers admired a rhetorical triumph. The *Albany Times-Union* said, "This is one of those rare speeches which progresses logically and powerfully from terse opening to challenging end." Kennedy's words, the newspaper predicted, "will be recalled and quoted so long as there are Americans to heed his summons to bear the burden of a long twilight struggle." The *Atlanta Constitution* observed, "There is an economy of style and a controlled power about this new president. They promise effect and vigor. Perhaps he really can lead us to light our country with such a faith that 'the glow from that fire can truly light the world.'" The *Denver Post* went further, finding in the speech the end of the sleepy fifties:

> This was a call to action which Americans have needed to hear for many years; its promise of leadership brought the warmth of hope, even on a cold day, that the Nation, under its new leadership, can rouse itself from the complacent aura of comfort that afflicts so many of us and tap more deeply than ever before our reservoir of profound strength and purpose.

Some even sought to praise Kennedy by adopting the speech's antipodal style. The *Baltimore Sun* called it "somber without despair, firm without bellicosity, bold without arrogance." The *New York Times* found "a tone of firmness but not of defiance, of dignity but not of pride, of generosity but not of servility, of reason but not of self-righteousness."

And that was just the first day.

On the day after the speech, the *Washington Post* quoted sixteen different United States senators praising it. William Proxmire of Wisconsin said the Kennedy address would rank with "Lincoln's and Franklin D. Roosevelt's inaugural address." As the columnists weighed in, the historical comparisons accelerated. Arthur Krock of the *New York Times*, who had assisted Kennedy in the editing and publication of *Why England Slept*, told the new president at a dinner party on the evening of inauguration day that the speech was the finest U.S. political document since Woodrow Wilson. Kennedy encouraged Krock to share that view, and Krock did so, writing for the Sunday *Times* that "in their delivery and rhetoric . . . Mr. Kennedy's [words] recalled Woodrow Wilson's first inaugural to this reporter, who viewed and heard both." James Reston, writing in the same newspaper on the same day, went a bit further:

> . . . as a speech it was remarkable, and maybe we ought to settle for the revival of the beauty of the English language. The evangelical and transcendental spirit of America has not been better expressed since Woodrow Wilson, and maybe not even since Ralph Waldo Emerson.

Walter Lippmann was almost alone in restraining himself, calling the speech "a remarkably successful piece of self-expression."

Kennedy's decision to ignore domestic issues was almost totally overlooked. Rowland Evans, reporting for the *New York Herald Tribune*, found Democrats well pleased with the speech. "Privately, however, there was some surprise at its failure to mention in passing any of the major domestic enterprises that Mr. Kennedy dealt with at length during the campaign." But the *Wall Street Journal*, which had been disappointed with the outcome of the 1960 election, found in this omission reason for hope. "The President not only failed to elaborate on the New Frontier here at home, he spoke as though he had never heard of it." From this, the *Journal* drew the conclusion that "there seems to us to be considerably less naiveté here than before."

While "ask not" has come to be the best-remembered passage in the speech, it was not clear at the time that this would be so. Senator Mike Monroney of Oklahoma, calling it "the best Inaugural Address I have heard in my lifetime," beginning with Wilson's second in 1917, singled out "let us never negotiate out of fear, but let us never fear to negotiate." French Ambassador Herve Alphand concurred. The editors of the *New York Times* considered the paragraph beginning "Let the word go forth . . ." to be the "Quotation of the Day." The editors of *Time* added the pledge to "bear any burden" to the list of "passages . . . of inspired and inspiring eloquence" which they compared to FDR's 1933 declaration that "The only thing we have to fear is fear itself."

Nor was what *Time* called "a surge of praise and congratulation" limited to journalists. On returning to his farm in South Salem, New York, from the ceremonies in Washington, former Vice President Henry Wallace wrote to Kennedy that first Sunday: "At no time in our history have so many tens of millions of people been so completely enthusiastic about an Inaugural Address as about yours." From his Maine farmhouse, E. B. White wrote, "I saw first the lectern take fire, then so much else—thanks to your brave words. I promise that whenever I can manage I'll blow my little draft of air on the beloved flame." From New York City, John Steinbeck, who, like Wallace, had attended the inauguration, wrote the president thanking him for the invitation to attend:

> I was profoundly moved by this ceremony which I had never seen before and even more moved by your following speech which was not only nobly conceived and excellently written and delivered, but also had that magic undertone of truth which cannot be simulated nor synchronized nor synthecized [sic] . . .
>
> Again my thanks, my pledge and my passionate hope that your words may become history.

And then Steinbeck added by hand, "And I believe they will!"* And from Tucson, Arizona, on Tuesday the 24th came a hand-

---

*Steinbeck's letter had made no reference to prayer, but Kennedy added the following handwritten postscript to his own form-letter response to letters about the inauguration from artists: "No President was ever prayed over with such fervor. Evidently they felt that the country or I needed it—probably both!"

written note from Eleanor Roosevelt, who seemed to have abandoned her skepticism:

> I wanted to tell you how I felt about your inaugural address. I
> think "gratitude" best describes the *kind* of liberation and lift
> to the listener which you gave. I have re-read your words
> several times and I am filled with thankfulness. May we all
> respond to your leadership and make your task easier.

On that same day, just four days after the inauguration,
Richard Walker, a teacher at Bronxville High School in
Bronxville, New York, where the Kennedy family had lived from
1929 to 1941, administered the first-semester final exam to his
third-year Latin students. Walker was "so excited by the eloquence, the Ciceronian rhetoric, the depth of historic perspective" of Kennedy's address that he translated its opening
sentences into Latin and had his students translate it back into
English as part of their test. In sending a copy of the test to
Kennedy, Walker's son wrote, "The students enjoyed it as much
as my father." Nor was Mr. Walker alone. In Portland, Maine,
Miss Eva Alley asked her thirty-two students of Cicero to translate passages from the Kennedy speech into Ciceronian Latin.
One of the students wrote the president that "Because of your
inaugural address, we juniors and seniors realize now that Latin
is not a dead language."*

---

*In response to an October 9, 1961, letter to Kennedy from Asher Rosen-
thal of Brooklyn, observing that the inaugural's "flow of words is almost ex-
actly the same as Cicero's *Oratio Prima in Catilinam*," Sorensen wrote on
Kennedy's behalf: "It is interesting to have your reaction to its style—that you
feel it might have been patterned after Cicero's writings. This was not a conscious effort on his part, I am sure."

Many years later, Garry Wills would claim that Kennedy's antecedents
were not Latin but Greek, drawing on the Funeral Orations of Gorgias. The
real point, no doubt, is that the rhetorical power of antithesis is timeless, and
has long been recognized as such.

This sort of popular enthusiasm, both for the new president and specifically for his first speech in his new office, was broad-based. In February and March 1961, Louis Harris and Associates, the president's pollsters, took soundings of opinion in the state of Kentucky and in the Seattle area, both places that had gone for Nixon the previous November, as a means toward gauging "Public Reaction to President Kennedy During the First 60 Days of His Administration." The survey found that the inaugural address had "made a profound impact." Favorable impressions of the speech remained with 81 percent of respondents in Kentucky and 83 percent of those in Seattle; "unfavorables" were only 6 percent in Kentucky and a mere 2 percent in Seattle. Among twelve specific actions or events tested, the inaugural address ranked highest in approval, ahead of Kennedy's press conferences and his State of the Union address, but also of such things as his minimum-wage proposals and his handling of the Soviet release of two Air Force pilots held since the preceding year. And the inaugural address was not only the most-approved of the administration's actions but also the most closely followed, with just 13 percent of those in Kentucky and 15 percent of those in Seattle saying they had "not followed" it.

Of course, it was not unanimous. Max Ascoli, editor of *The Reporter* magazine, was deeply skeptical. He denied being either "impressed or stirred" by the speech, and wrote that "sentences like 'let us never negotiate out of fear. But let us never fear to negotiate' bear the evidence of [a] lyrical prose, of [a] spiritual hiccough." When Kennedy received Ascoli for lunch in February 1961, even this slender bit of criticism had been enough to sting him. The new president greeted the editor with, "You didn't like my inaugural." Ascoli claimed, "It's not the speech, it's the genre." "By your standards, then," Kennedy rejoined, "how would you judge Lincoln's Gettysburg Address?" "I have never liked that either," Ascoli said. Kennedy seemed satisfied, not with Ascoli but with the standard.

Little of this, of course, concerned the *policies* advanced in the speech. But some did notice the implications of the address for substance as well as style. James Reston's column in the *New York Times* the morning after the address observed that "American idealism has now been allied to American power." Of "ask not," Reston said, "Whatever else this means, it surely does not mean less national service, or lower taxes, or higher wages, or greater profits, or more protection against imports."

The columnist Max Lerner went further and looked more closely into the heart of the address. He concluded that Kennedy had committed the nation to arms-control negotiations. At the same time Lerner foresaw "no letup in the world political war," but with that war pursued primarily by "nonmilitary," ideological means.

✿ As the years went on, the Kennedy inaugural itself became an ideological touchstone.

During his lifetime, President Kennedy promoted this talismanic quality for the speech by occasionally quoting it himself, always without attribution. In 1961, eulogizing Secretary General Dag Hammarskjold before the United Nations General Assembly, Kennedy said, "I pledge you . . . that we shall never negotiate out of fear, we shall never fear to negotiate." Later in the same speech, he (again) envisioned an age "in which the strong are just and the weak secure and the peace preserved." Less than eight weeks later, speaking at the University of Washington in Seattle, he attacked those on the right "who cannot bear the burden of a long twilight struggle." Playing on his own phrase, he declared that "while we shall negotiate freely, we shall not negotiate freedom."

On the first anniversary of the inauguration, at a Democratic National Committee fund-raising dinner at the National Guard Armory in Washington, Kennedy repeated this pattern, speaking of "those who would make themselves our adversaries," and ending his remarks with the injunction that "the fire from our effort can light the world." But beyond these two serious references, Kennedy permitted himself a brief self-parody, saying he "would like to paraphrase a couple of statements" from the inaugural:

> . . . *we observe tonight not a celebration of freedom but a victory of party, for we have sworn to pay off the same party debt our forebears ran up nearly a year and three months ago.*
>
> *Our deficit will not be paid off in the next hundred days, nor will it be paid off in the first one thousand days, nor in the life of this administration. Nor even perhaps in our lifetime on this planet, but let us begin—remembering that generosity is not a sign of weakness and that Ambassadors are always subject to Senate confirmation, for if the Democratic Party cannot be helped by the many who are poor, it cannot be saved by the few who are rich. So let us begin.*

The crowd roared with laughter, and the evening took its place in the annals of Kennedy wit.

But the 125-word parody passage was actually only a small portion of a nearly 700-word complete parody address that Sorensen had proposed for the occasion. The entire Sorensen draft parody is reproduced in Appendix G. As a whole, it was much harder-edged, much more partisan than the portions Kennedy used. Sorensen's draft declared near the outset,

> *But let every Republican know, whether he wishes us well or ill, that we shall pay any price, bear any burden, meet any hardship, support any friend, oppose any foe to assure the survival and the success of our Party.*

The political appeal was raw:

We dare not neglect our own majorities. For only when we have votes sufficient beyond doubt can we be certain beyond doubt that they will never be needed in a roll-call.

Even the most stirring passages of the original speech were included:

*Now the Chairman summons us again—not as a call to cast votes, though votes we need—not as a call to man the polls, though polls we are taking—but a call to bear the financial burden of a long political struggle, year in and year out—a struggle against the common enemies of all Democrats: Miller, Goldwater, Rockefeller, and Nixon himself.**

And, finally,

And so, my fellow Democrats: Ask not what your party can give to you—ask what you can give to your party.

Let us never contribute to our own decline. But let us never decline to contribute.

Sorensen says the idea for such a parody "probably grew out of a conversation" he had with the president, and he remembers Kennedy laughing over the full draft. But "Bobby [Kennedy] was there, saying, 'No, it's sacrilege.' He didn't want him to do it. And that may be why it was cut." Robert Kennedy's view was, perhaps, the long one. It is Sorensen, after all, who now observes

*Miller was Representative William Miller of New York, later the 1964 Republican vice-presidential nominee, but at this time chairman of the Republican National Committee. Sorensen notes the choice of three names ending in "er" as part of his fondness for doggerel. It may also have been intended to evoke FDR's famous 1940 attack on isolationist Republicans "Martin, Barton, and Fish."

that some people find the words of the martyred president's inaugural "holy."

ᔓ While Kennedy lived, however, others shared Sorensen's instinct that the inaugural could be a source of fun. On Kennedy's 1963 trip to Germany, while riding into Wiesbaden, which housed a large American base, the motorcade passed a sign saying, "Ask Not What You Can Do for Your Ford Dealer, Ask What Your Ford Dealer Can Do for You."

But that tone vanished, of course, after Dallas.

The prayer card at President Kennedy's funeral was simple and elegant. It contained his name, picture, title, dates of birth and death, the words "Dear God, Please take care of your servant, John Fitzgerald Kennedy," and the following quotation:

> *Now the trumpet summons us again—not as a call to arms, though arms we need—not as a call to battle, though embattled we are—but a call to bear the burden of a long, twilight struggle, year in and year out, "rejoicing in hope, patient in tribulation"—a struggle against the common enemies of man: tyranny, poverty, disease and war itself. . . .*
>
> *In the long history of the world, only a few generations have been granted the role of defending freedom in its hour of maximum danger. I do not shrink from this responsibility—I welcome it. I do not believe that any of us would exchange places with any other people or any other generation. The energy, the faith, the devotion which we bring to this endeavor will light our country and all who serve it—and the glow from that fire can truly light the world. . . .*
>
> *With a good conscience our only sure reward, with history the final judge of our deeds, let us go forth to lead the land we love, asking His blessing and His help, but knowing that here on earth God's work must truly be our own.*

At the conclusion of the funeral's low mass, the auxiliary bishop of Washington read aloud the entire inaugural address.

When later the temporary gravesite in Arlington National Cemetery was remodeled and made permanent, the following inscription, beyond his name and the years of his life—and set as if in verse—was the only one placed there:

Let the word go forth
From this time and place
To friend and foe alike
That the torch has been passed
To a new generation of Americans.

Let every nation know
Whether it wishes us well or ill
That we shall pay any price—bear any burden
Meet any hardship—support any friend
Oppose any foe to assure the survival
And the success of liberty

Now the trumpet summons us again
Not as a call to arms
—though arms we need
Not as a call to battle
—though embattled we are
But a call to bear the burden of a long, twilight struggle
A struggle against the common enemies of man
Tyranny–Poverty–Disease—and War itself

In the long history of the world
Only a few generations have been granted
The role of defending freedom
In its hour of maximum danger

I do not shrink from this responsibility
I welcome it

The energy—the Faith—the Devotion
Which we bring to this endeavor
Will light our country
And all who serve it
And the glow from that fire
Can truly light the world

And so my fellow Americans
Ask not what your country can do for you
Ask what you can do for your country
My fellow citizens of the world—ask not
What America can do for you—but what together
We can do for the freedom of man

With a good conscience our only sure reward
With history the final judge of our deeds
Let us go forth to lead the land we love—asking His blessing
And His help—but knowing that here on earth
God's work must truly be our own.

The canonization of John Kennedy had begun, and the in-augural address was put forward as the first of his miracles. When Great Britain dedicated its memorial to Kennedy, an acre of meadow at Runnymede, the marker also bore the inscription of Kennedy's vow to "pay any price, bear any burden." That same year saw the historian Samuel Eliot Morison write, "There had been no inaugural address like this since Lincoln's second." And a leading journal of rhetoric would agree that that "summarized the sentiment of most scholars."

The "memorabilia" version of the inaugural address had first gone on public display just six months after the assassination, as part of a preview of an eventual Kennedy Library. Jacqueline Kennedy whispered to reporters, "I suppose the photographs are the hardest to look at. And perhaps his inaugural address in his own handwriting." Some years later, nearly as Kennedy had imagined, a handwritten sheet containing the "ask not" passage that he had copied out at the request of a friend, sold at auction for $11,000, at that time the highest price ever paid for a letter by any president since Lincoln.*

❧ But the tumult of the late sixties began to cloud the consensus surrounding the legacy of the inaugural. As early as 1964, the scholar William Carleton, writing in the *Antioch Review*, called the inaugural address "alarmist, already historically off key, more suited to the Stalinist era than to 1961." The 1963 American University speech on peace, Carleton predicted, "will be remembered long after Kennedy's inaugural address is forgotten." Critiques came from both left and right, especially in light of the failure of the American adventure in Vietnam. From the left, George McGovern, a Kennedy administration subcabinet officer, became the Democratic nominee in 1972. McGovern later expressed his disillusionment this way: "The president had raised the standard pretty high in his inaugural address—the business of bearing any burden and taking on any foe was great at the time, but looking back on it, I think it was really quite arrogant and extravagant in assuming any one country had the right to do that."

Henry Fairlie's 1973 book *The Kennedy Promise* summed up the disappointment. Of the inaugural address, Fairlie wrote, "It

---

*In 1998 a piece of paper on which Kennedy had scribbled the first few words of the "memorabilia" version of the inaugural, only to then start over, brought $39,000. Evelyn Lincoln had retrieved the scrap from the trash and bequeathed it to a friend.

was brilliant; it was moving; it was dangerous." In particular, the left seized on the same commitment to which McGovern referred (and which Fairlie's native Britain had celebrated)—the vow to "pay any price, bear any burden, meet any hardship, support any friend, oppose any foe"—as the intellectual battle cry of the Vietnam debacle. Fairlie wrote,

> These are the words which many of those who applauded the speech at the time now find offensive; and they are offensive. By what right does a leader of any free people commit them—for it was a commitment which he was making— to "pay *any* price, bear *any* burden, meet *any* hardship," when their country is not even at war, and not directly threatened? . . . The commitment that John Kennedy was making on a conspicuous stage was without limit.

The key phrase in this critique is "when their country is . . . not directly threatened." From the right, in the person of Kennedy's old adversary, Richard Nixon—now elected president in the wake of the failure of the Kennedy-Johnson Vietnam policy—came a different but equally critical perspective. Where Kennedy, building on American strength and his own sense of urgency, had confronted the Soviets, even as he occasionally talked of accommodation, Nixon, working from what he and Henry Kissinger saw as American weakness, sought détente with the Soviets, even as he occasionally talked of confrontation. Both presidents considered themselves realists in a world surfeited with romantics, and, wrote former Nixon aide William Safire, "Nixon's standard as a modern President, conscious or not, was John F. Kennedy."

In his own second inaugural address in 1973, at the height of his power, with peace in Vietnam at hand and Watergate seemingly a blip on the previous election year's radar, Nixon took

Kennedy on directly. And he did so not only on America's role in the world but on government's role in America. In the course of his speech, without mentioning Kennedy by name, Nixon three times turned Kennedy's words inside out:

> The time has passed when America will make every other nation's conflict our own, or make every other nation's future our responsibility, or presume to tell the people of other nations how to manage their own affairs.

> Let us build a structure of peace in the world in which the weak are as safe as the strong—in which each respects the right of the other to live by a different system—in which those who would influence others will do so by the strength of their ideas, and not by the force of their arms.

> In our own lives, let each of us ask—not just what will government do for me, but what can I do for myself?
> In the challenges we face together, let each of us ask— not just how can government help, but how can I help?*

In the mid-seventies and beyond, however, as Nixon himself was hounded by the left (and finally abandoned by the center), and his détente discredited on the right, Kennedy's inaugural seemed to enjoy something of a resurgence. Or, perhaps to put it more precisely, the speech seemed to pass from partisan debate to become part of the basic American text.

---

*This last point of Nixon's draws on Milton Friedman's 1962 critique in *Capitalism and Freedom*, where Friedman wrote: "The free man will ask neither what his country can do for him nor what he can do for his country. He will ask rather 'What can I and my compatriots do through government to help discharge our responsibilities to achieve our several goals and purposes, and above all, to protect our freedom?' And he will accompany this question with another: How can we keep the government from becoming a Franken-stein that will destroy the very freedom we establish it to protect?"

In 1984, President Ronald Reagan cited Kennedy's "long twilight struggle" in support of his own Central American policy. Kennedy, Reagan declared, "understood the problem of Central America. He understood Castro. And he understood the long-term goals of the Soviet Union in this region. . . . Were John Kennedy alive today, I think he would be appalled by the gullibility of some who invoke his name." Running to succeed Reagan in 1988, and in opposition to most Reagan policies, Massachusetts Governor Michael Dukakis promised to "pay any price, bear any burden," and all the rest. And Dukakis took to urging audiences all over the country to "Ask more of your candidates, because the next president will be asking more of you." Among the men Dukakis defeated for the Democratic nomination, Representative Richard Gephardt told an Iowa campaign audience, "Let every nation know, friend or foe, that we are ready to meet any economic challenge, to modernize any industry, to marshal all of our talents and all of our toughness to ensure the success of the American economy." And Senator Joseph Biden said, "In the spirit of another time, let us pledge that our generation of Americans will pay any price, bear any burden, accept any challenge, meet any hardship to secure the blessings of prosperity and the promise of America for our children."

Of John Kennedy, the political consultant Robert Squier observed, "He is the Bureau of Standards for this generation of Democrats. The quick way to define yourself is in relation to him." Bill Clinton, on the day before his presidency began, made a public pilgrimage to Kennedy's grave. Then he quoted Kennedy's inaugural peroration at his first annual Washington prayer breakfast. But Kennedy was a touchstone not only for Democrats. President George H. W. Bush in his 1991 State of the Union address referred to bearing "the burden of leadership" in a post–cold war world. Many observers thought the predecessor he was most nearly trying to evoke was Kennedy. And the same peroration quoted by Clinton in 1993 provided the conclusion for Representative J. C. Watts's Republican rebuttal to Clinton's 1997 State of the Union.

By late 1992, Kennedy's inaugural address had achieved such iconic status that Richard Holbrooke could tell of spending Christmas Eve in Bangkok listening "to a Thai businessman demonstrate his love of the United States by reciting [it] to us, word for word."

Kennedy's words had entered global political discourse. In his first speech as president-elect of South Africa, Nelson Mandela noted that "Today we celebrate not a victory of party, but a victory for all the people." And South Africa's Methodist bishop, urging self-reliance, warned, "Ask not what America can do for you." Taking office in Israel in 1996, Prime Minister Benjamin Netanyahu said the "torch has been passed" to a new generation.

✍ In all, a divide opened—and widened—between the place Kennedy's inaugural address holds in the memory of the people of the United States and the world (and the politicians who seek to appeal to them), on the one hand, and scholars on the other. The scholarly consensus of 1966, ranking anything to do with Kennedy along with Lincoln, has long since dissolved. But Kennedy's place in popular memory is undimmed.

In 1988, twenty-five years after his assassination, a survey of schoolchildren by *Scholastic* magazine ranked Kennedy second only to Lincoln among American presidents, just ahead of Franklin Roosevelt. At the same time a survey of historians agreed that Lincoln stood first but placed Kennedy thirteenth. One of the historians also predicted that Kennedy's reputation would continue to decline and that "it will take about 20 or 30 more years to get an analytical viewpoint on his era." He added, "However, anybody that hears [Kennedy's inaugural] and doesn't have some stirring in his soul is probably lacking poetry in his heart. Kennedy's symbolic stature is never going to decline—no one can take that away from him."

The public at large has certainly continued to feel the stirring. In a 1983 Gallup survey, 44 percent of Americans ranked Kennedy a "good" president, and 31 percent a "great" one. Ten years later, the numbers had actually improved, with 38 percent ranking him good, and 41 percent "great." A 1987 ABC News / Washington Post survey found Kennedy well ahead as the president who did the best job "in your lifetime." A 1991 Gallup survey of adults replicated the 1988 findings among children, with Kennedy ranked just behind Lincoln as the "greatest" president in the country's history.

When the subject shifted from perceptions of "greatness" to those of "effectiveness" or other dimensions, the picture was a bit more mixed—but only a bit. An NBC / Wall Street Journal poll taken the week that Reagan's eight years as president were ending found Kennedy just ahead of the departing chief executive in a ranking of "most effective" post–World War II presidents. But both Kennedy and Reagan ranked well ahead of Harry Truman, Dwight Eisenhower, and the others. Reagan actually edged Kennedy in a 1994 survey that asked, "Of all the U.S. presidents who have been elected since you first started following politics, which one do you think has done the best job?" But this may well have been because, if the question were interpreted literally, only those respondents over the age of roughly forty-five would have been eligible to choose Kennedy while nearly all respondents could have picked Reagan.* Kennedy still placed second,

---

*Similarly, a 1987 survey asked, "Which president that you voted for do you believe will prove to have the greatest impact on American history?" Kennedy ranked second to Reagan, then the incumbent. In 1987 no one under the age of forty-eight could have voted for Kennedy.

well ahead of George H. W. Bush, who had left office only the year before, and of Bill Clinton, the then-incumbent who defeated Bush.

Most recently, when asked in 1998 to express job approval or disapproval of past presidents on the basis of "what you have heard, read, or remember," Kennedy scored highest on approval at 77 percent and lowest on disapproval at 17 percent. And a 2004 Gallup survey ranked Kennedy first among modern presidents, just ahead of FDR, with nearly 80 percent terming him "outstanding" or "above average."

But just as the public continued to be moved, scholars remain unmoved. A 2003 nonpartisan survey of scholars on historical presidential leadership by the *Wall Street Journal* and the Federalist Society ranked Kennedy eighteenth, at the bottom of the group of "above average" presidents. Both his immediate predecessor, Eisenhower, and his immediate successor, Lyndon Johnson, ranked ahead of him. So did Reagan and Truman—and William McKinley. Moreover, the editors of the survey reported,

> there was a shocking consensus on the most overrated president: John Kennedy. When the opportunity to name the most overrated presidents arose, 43 of the 78 scholars named Kennedy. That a solid majority would volunteer his name suggests that his reputation is falling. Indeed, sometimes viewed in the category of the "near great," JFK has now dropped into the bottom of the "above average" group.

The author (and sometime Republican presidential speech-writer) Peggy Noonan concludes:

> History will take a cool-eyed look at John F. Kennedy and his accomplishments and failures only when all who were alive when he was alive are gone. . . .

The numerically biggest generation in all American history was at its most impressionable when he was the most lionized, in the years after his death. Boomers now run the world. It doesn't matter what they know of JFK now, as adults, or what they've learned. They're not going to shake their sense that he was King Arthur lost upon the field. They're not going to let you shake it, either.

Noonan is a member of that generation (as, to be sure, is the author of this book). She has "seen through" Kennedy and believes that, once the metaphor of the Exodus is relived, others will as well.

But there are reasons to believe she is wrong, that her own politics are blinding her to the ways in which Kennedy is coming to transcend politics. Some of the evidence for this is present in the polling data just reviewed: the strong, positive views of Kennedy clearly already extend to those not born during Kennedy's lifetime. They are already beginning to pass them down to their own children. What is fading about Kennedy is not his image but the divisions surrounding his policies, and their consequences, and even his lifestyle. He has been dead now more than forty years; he is a more distant memory for us than Woodrow Wilson or Theodore Roosevelt were for him, or than the last surviving Framers were for Lincoln. Yet Kennedy endures in the popular imagination, a consensus figure now as he never was in life, much (in that respect) like Lincoln or Franklin Roosevelt before him. Why?

The answer, or at least a significant measure of it, I would submit, is what this book has been about. The enduring power of John Kennedy's appeal stems importantly from his speeches, and especially from his inaugural address. And television—then and now—ensures that that appeal endures, and will endure.

This is, after all, the one aspect of Kennedy on which scholars and the general public agree. Thus, in the year 2000, a television critic for a metropolitan tabloid—certainly not an intellectual pulpit—declared that Kennedy's inaugural address was the second greatest speech in the history of television, trailing only Dr. Martin Luther King, Jr.'s "I Have a Dream" speech at the March on Washington in August 1963. Three years later a survey of 137 scholars asked them to name the greatest American speeches of the twentieth century, based on the criteria of historical impact and rhetorical artistry. Again Kennedy's inaugural followed only King's "I Have a Dream." The only other inaugural address on the list of the ten greatest speeches was FDR's first inaugural, which was ranked third overall.

The last thought on this subject fittingly belongs to Theodore Sorensen. Decades after Kennedy's death, Sorensen edited a volume of Kennedy's speeches, statements, and writings. Sorensen began his own introduction to that volume by noting of Kennedy, "He believed in the power and glory of words—both written and spoken—to win votes, to set goals, to change minds, to move nations." Today, as America again needs to move nations, it is the power and the glory of his words—whatever their source—that has sustained John F. Kennedy as a political force into a new century. They are likely to do so through the whole history of the land he loved.

Appendices

The Surviving Excerpts from the First Draft of Kennedy's Inaugural Address

We celebrate today not a victory of party but the sacrament of democracy—a ceremony of peaceful change and renewal.

Each of us, whether we hold office or not, shares the responsibility for guiding this most difficult of all societies along the path of self-discipline and self-government.

Nor can two great and powerful nations forever continue on this reckless course, both overburdened by the staggering cost of modern weapons. . . .

And if the fruits of cooperation prove sweeter than the dregs of suspicion, let both sides join ultimately in creating a true world order—neither a Pax Americana nor a Pax Russiana, nor even a balance of power—but a community of power where the strong are just and the weak secure and the rule of law maintained.

The Earliest Surviving Draft of the Address— The Cut-down Version of the TCS Draft, on or before January 10, 1961

[first page missing]

So let the word go forth to all the world—and suit the action to the word—that this generation of Americans has no intention of becoming soft instead of resolute, smug instead of resourceful, or citizens of a second-rate power. Like Patrick Henry in a similar hour, we are willing, "whatever anguish of spirit it may cost . . . to know the whole truth, to know the worst and to provide for it."

And the worst is fast upon us, with the threat of hostile power growing in every corner of our planet. There is not a continent, not a country, not a city where the enemies of freedom have not extended their hidden or open assaults.

Yet our alliances in the West are unfulfilled and insecure. Our neighbors to the South are torn by pressures from within and without. Our friends in less-developed states are diverting resources we are loath to replace into useless power struggles.

Meanwhile, the grand organization for peace we helped create withers into little more than a forum for invective. The dread secret of the atom we first unlocked spreads slowly, but all too swiftly, around a globe hell-bent for planned or accidental suicide. The instruments of war have far outpaced the instruments of peace.

At this very hour, as we share this ceremony of peaceful change and renewal, there are other voices heard in other lands— some threatening, some despairing, some urging a slow retreat.

But let every nation know, be it friend or foe, that we shall not yield to threat or force in our vow to keep the peace—that we intend to stand by our commitments—and that we are prepared to do whatever must be done to assure freedom's success and survival.

This much we pledge and more.

To those old allies whose cultural and spiritual origins we share, we pledge the loyalty of faithful friends. United, there is little we cannot do in a host of new joint ventures. Divided, there is little we can do—for we dare not meet a powerful foe at odds and split asunder.

To those new states we now welcome to the ranks of the free, we pledge our word that one form of colonial control shall not have passed merely to be replaced by a far more iron tyranny. We shall not always expect to find you on our side. But we shall always expect to find you vigorously on the side of your own freedom—and to know that those who foolishly seek power by riding on the tiger's back inevitably end up inside.

To those peoples in the huts and villages of half the globe struggling to break the bonds of mass misery, we pledge our best efforts to help you help yourselves, for whatever period is required—not because our enemies are doing it, not because we seek your votes, but because it is right. If freedom's way cannot help the many who are poor, it can never save the few who are rich.

To our sister republics south of our border, a special pledge—to convert at last our good words into good deeds—to assist free men and free governments in casting off the chains of poverty. But this peaceful revolution of hope must not become and shall not become the tool of hostile powers. Let every neighbor know that we shall join to prevent aggression or subversion anywhere in the Americas. And let every other power know that this Hemisphere intends to remain master of its own house.

To that world assembly of sovereign states, the last best hope on earth, we renew our pledge of support—to strengthen its shield of the new and the weak—and to enlarge the area to which its writ may run.

Finally, to those nations who make themselves our enemy, we offer not a pledge but a sincere request: that both sides begin anew the quest for peace, before the dark powers of destruction unleashed by science engulf us all in ruin.

We dare not tempt you with weakness. For only when our arms are sufficient beyond doubt can we be certain beyond doubt that they will never be employed.

But neither can two great and powerful nations long endure their present reckless course, both overburdened by the staggering cost of modern weapons, both rightly alarmed by the steady spread of the deadly atom, yet both racing to alter that uncertain balance of terror that stays the hand of mankind's final war.

So let us begin anew—remembering on both sides that civility is not a sign of weakness, and that sincerity is always subject to proof. Let us never negotiate out of fear. But let us never fear to negotiate.

Let both sides explore what problems unite us instead of belaboring what problems divide us.

Let both sides, for the first time, formulate serious and precise proposals for the inspection and control of arms—and bring

the absolute power to destroy other nations under the absolute control of all nations.

Let both sides unite to heed the command of Isaiah—"to undo the heavy burdens, to let the oppressed go free." Together let us explore the stars, conquer the deserts, feed the hungry, eradicate disease, tap the ocean depths and encourage the arts and commerce.

And if a beach-head of cooperation can push back the jungles of suspicion, let both sides join some day in creating, not a new balance of power, but a new world of law, where the strong are just and the weak secure and the peace preserved forever.

All this will not be finished in the first one hundred days. Nor will it be finished in the first one thousand days, nor in the life of this Administration, nor even perhaps in our life-time on this planet.

But let us begin—with short realistic steps—but with high idealistic vision—determined that our wish for public praise will never blur our sense of public duty—determined that we will master our affairs before they can master us.

Will our hearts and minds be clear enough to see our duty? Will our spirit and will be strong enough to try?

In your hands, my fellow citizens, more than mine, lie the final answer. Were we to suffer open armed attack, our decision would be clear, our response instant, our dedication to the cause complete. We would not pause to count the cost or weigh the odds. We would not heed the voices of surrender, fear or panic. Every man and every woman would answer the call of the trumpet.

Today the trumpet sounds its urgent call again—not a call to arms, though arms we need—not a call to battle though embattled we are—but a call to a broader, more basic struggle against all the enemies of man—tyranny and poverty and war itself.

Will you join heart and soul in that historic battle? Will you give to the defense of self-government the same full measure of self-denial you would give to the fight for self-survival?

If we fail now, we fail our heirs, our forebears and all mankind. But if we prevail—if at the end of the tunnel of darkness we find the light—then we shall fulfill the dreams of those who love this land most not for what it was, not for what it is, but for what it can and will someday be.

So ask not what your country is going to do for you. Ask what you can do for your country. Ask of your leaders the same high standards and sacrifice that we will ask of you. And ask the Lord above to grant us all the strength and wisdom we shall need. [handwritten: With a clear conscience our only sure reward, with history the final judge of our motives, let us go forth to lead the land we love, asking his blessing and help, but knowing that here on earth God's work must truly be our own.]

APPENDIX C

Kennedy's Dictation, January 10, 1961

[Note: This is a rough transcription of Gregg shorthand taken by Mrs. Evelyn Lincoln, John Kennedy's personal secretary. While Mrs. Lincoln typed up a transcript herself just after taking this dictation, neither that transcription nor any other survives. The acknowledgments include gratitude for assistance with creating this transcription—the author of the present book has no training in shorthand—but responsibility for this version remains with the author.]

The inaugural is an end as well as a beginning. Today we are linked with thirty-five other Americans, three who are with us, who stood in the same place, took the same oath, made the same commitment for the preservation of the American Constitution that I have made today.

We are a young people but are an older republic. But though we are older at least as the life of political systems are measured, we must not forget that we are descendants of revolutionaries. We stand in succession of five men: Washington, Adams, Jefferson, Madison, and Monroe, participating in a more drastic and far-reaching time than any that now seems [———] have legitimized or marked with doctrines as they were two centuries ago. The concept of the rights of man come not from the generosity of the state but the hand of God.

I hope the order will go out from this place to a watching world that a new generation of Americans—born in this century, tempered by the war, have come to positions of power in this great republic. And I hope those who wish us well, and those who wish us ill, will understand that we do not plan to participate in or witness the defeat of the revolutionary concepts to which this country has always been committed and which are now at issue in the world struggle. The plans for which our ancestors fought here, we fight for around the globe.

And we shall pay any price, bear any burden, meet any hardships, support any friend, oppose any foe in order to maintain this rich heritage. This much we pledge and more.

p. 3, 4, 5, page (separate) 6

In this crucial decade the sixties may well earn the success or failure of the cause. We sail today on seas on subterranean explosions—by currents which, twisting and turning, threaten to engulf us [———]

But we sail in confidence in the fixed stars that guided us to our present power. The desire for peace, but peace with freedom. The desire for prosperity in which others share—a belief in God—but with respect to the beliefs of others, not just on our voyage at sea. In short, we seek circumstances which will make peace for all mankind.

In your hands, fellow citizens, more than mine lies the final answer. Since this country was founded, every generation of Americans has been called at least once to give testimony to their national loyalty.

The graves of young Americans who responded circle the globe, now throughout a wide [———]. We know we are not prepared to slide and drift into defeat, and we know Americans are ready once more to pay the price of maintaining their freedom. Obviously the price may not be a just quick sacrifice of war, rather it may be our fate particularly to bear the burden of action in order to win this twilight struggle. Today we sound the trumpet once again, not as a call to arms, though arms we need, not as a call to battle, though embattled we are, rather a call for a broader, deeper struggle against the common enemies of man: tyranny, poverty, disease, and war itself.

Can we forge against these enemies a great alliance, North and South, East and West, can we assure a more fruitful life for all mankind. A few generations has it been given in the long history of the world who have been chosen to be a people defender of freedom at a time of maximum danger. I do not shrink from this responsibility—I welcome it. I do not believe we should change places with any other people or any other generations. The energy may be confidence and devotion and by the call of freedom with all of us who serve it—and the glow in a fire would light the world.

My fellow Americans: ask not what your country will do for you, ask rather what you can do for your country. My fellow citizens of the world, ask not what America or any other country will do for you, but rather what you yourself can do for freedom. You ask of us the same high standards of sacrifice and comradeship. We seek from you and [———] we shall lift the world

APPENDIX D

The Penultimate Draft of the Address, January 17, 1961

My Fellow-Citizens:

We celebrate today not a victory of party but a convention of freedom—symbolizing an end as well as a beginning—signifying renewal as well as change. For I have sworn before you and Almighty God the same solemn oath our forebears prescribed nearly a century and three-quarters ago.

The world is very different now—empowered as it is to banish all form of human poverty and all form of human life. And yet the same revolutionary concepts for which those forebears fought are still at issue around the globe—the concept that the rights of man come not from the generosity of the state but from the hand of God.

We dare not forget today that we are the heirs of that first revolution. Let the word go forth from this time and place, to friend and foe alike, that the torch of liberty has been passed to a new generation of Americans—born in this century, baptized by war, disciplined by a cold and bitter peace, but proud of our ancient heritage—and unwilling to witness or permit the slow undoing of those same concepts of human rights to which this nation has always been committed, and to which we are committed today.

Let every nation know, whether it wish us well or ill, that we shall pay any price, bear any burden, meet any hardship, support any friend or oppose any foe in order to assure the survival and success of freedom.

This much we pledge—and more.

To those old allies whose cultural and spiritual origins we share, we pledge the loyalty of faithful friends. United, there is little we cannot do in a host of new joint ventures. Divided, there is little we can do—for we dare not meet a powerful foe at odds and split asunder.

To those new states whom we now welcome to the ranks of the free, we pledge our word that one form of colonial control shall not have passed merely to be replaced by a far more iron tyranny. We shall not always expect to find you on our side. But we shall always expect to find you vigorously on the side of your own freedom—and to they [sic, probably a typo; should be "remember"] that those who foolishly seek power by riding on the tiger's back inevitably end up inside.

To those people in the huts and villages of half the globe struggling to break the bonds of mass misery, we pledge our best efforts to help you help yourselves, for whatever period is required—not because our enemies are doing it, not because we seek your votes, but because it is right. If freedom's way cannot help the many who are poor, it can never save the few who are rich.

To our sister republics south of our border, a special pledge—to convert at last our good words into good deeds—in a new alliance for progress—to assist free men and free governments in casting off the chains of poverty. But your peaceful revolution of hope must not become the tool of hostile powers.

Let every neighbor know that we shall join to prevent aggression or subversion anywhere in the Americas. And let every other power know that this Hemisphere intends to remain master of its own house.

To that world assembly of sovereign states, the last best hope on earth—in an age where the instruments of war have far outpaced the instruments of peace—we renew our pledge of support—to make it more than a forum for invective—to strengthen its shield of the new and the weak—and to enlarge the area to which its writ may run.

Finally, to those nations who make themselves our enemy, we offer not a pledge but a request: that both sides begin anew the quest for peace, before the dark powers of destruction unleashed by science engulf all humanity in planned or accidental self-destruction.

We dare not tempt you with weakness. For only when our arms are sufficient beyond doubt can we be certain beyond doubt that they will never be employed.

But neither can two great and powerful nations long endure their present reckless course, both overburdened by the staggering cost of modern weapons, both rightly alarmed by the steady spread of the deadly atom, yet both racing to alter that uncertain balance of terror that stays the hand of mankind's final war.

So let us begin anew—remembering on both sides that civility is not a sign of weakness, and sincerity is always subject to proof. Let us never negotiate out of fear. But let us never fear to negotiate.

Let both sides explore what problems unite us instead of belaboring what problems divide us.

Let both sides, for the first time, formulate serious and precise proposals for the inspection and control of arms—and bring

the absolute power to destroy other nations under the absolute control of all nations.

Let both sides join to invoke the wonders of science instead of its terrors. Together let us explore the stars, conquer the deserts, eradicate disease, tap the ocean depths and encourage the arts and commerce.

Let both sides unite to heed in all corners of the earth the command of Isaiah—to ". . . loose the fetters of wickedness . . . undo the heavy burdens . . . let the oppressed go free . . . deal thy bread to the hungry . . . bring the poor into thy house . . . (For) then shall thy light break forth as the morning. . . ."

And if a beach-head of cooperation can push back the jungles of suspicion, let both sides join some day in creating, not a new balance of power, but a new world of law, where the strong are just and the weak secure and the peace preserved forever.

All this will not be finished in the first one hundred days. Nor will it be finished in the first one thousand days, nor in the life of this Administration, nor even perhaps in our life-time on this planet. But let us begin.

In your hands, my fellow citizens, more than mine, will be determined the success or failure of our course. Since this country was founded, each generation has been summoned to give testimony to its national loyalty. The graves of young Americans who answered that call encircle the globe.

Now the trumpet summons us again—not as a call to bear arms, though arms we need—not as a call to battle, though embattled we are—but a call to bear the burden of a long twilight struggle, year in and year out, "rejoicing in hope, patient in tribulation"—a struggle against the common enemies of war [sic, a typo; should be "man"]: tyranny, poverty, disease and war itself.

Can we forge against these enemies a grand and global alliance, North and South, East and West, that can assure a more fruitful life for all mankind? Will you join in that historic effort?

To few generations in the long history of the world have time and events granted the role of chief defenders of freedom at an hour of maximum danger. I do not shrink from this responsibility—I welcome it—and I do not believe that any of us would exchange places with any other people or any other generation. The energy, the faith and the devotion which we bring to this endeavor will light our country and all who serve it—and the glow from that fire can truly light the world. For "when a man's ways please the Lord, he maketh even his enemies to be at peace with him."

And so, my fellow Americans: ask not what your country will do for you—ask what you can do for your country.

My fellow citizens of the world: ask not what America will do for you, but what you can do for freedom.

Finally, whether you are citizens of America or the world, ask of me and those who serve with me the same high standards of strength and sacrifice that we will ask of you, while asking the Lord above to grant us all the strength and wisdom we shall need. With a good conscience our only sure reward, with history the final judge of our deeds, let us go forth to lead the land we love, asking His blessing and help, but knowing that here on earth God's work must truly be our own.

President Kennedy's Inaugural Address as Delivered, January 20, 1961

Vice President Johnson, Mr. Speaker, Mr. Chief Justice, President Eisenhower, Vice President Nixon, President Truman, reverend clergy, fellow citizens, we observe today not a victory of party, but a celebration of freedom—symbolizing an end, as well as a beginning—signifying renewal, as well as change. For I have sworn before you and Almighty God the same solemn oath our forebears prescribed nearly a century and three quarters ago.

The world is very different now. For man holds in his mortal hands the power to abolish all forms of human poverty and all forms of human life. And yet the same revolutionary beliefs for which our forebears fought are still at issue around the globe—the belief that the rights of man come not from the generosity of the state, but from the hand of God.

We dare not forget today that we are the heirs of that first revolution. Let the word go forth from this time and place, to friend and foe alike, that the torch has been passed to a new generation of Americans—born in this century, tempered by war, disciplined by a hard and bitter peace, proud of our ancient heritage—and unwilling to witness or permit the slow undoing of those human rights to which this Nation has always been committed, and to which we are committed today at home and around the world. [brief applause]

Let every nation know, whether it wishes us well or ill, that we shall pay any price, bear any burden, meet any hardship, support any friend, oppose any foe, to assure the survival and the success of liberty. [applause]

This much we pledge—and more.

To those old allies whose cultural and spiritual origins we share, we pledge the loyalty of faithful friends. United, there is little we cannot do in a host of cooperative ventures. Divided, there is little we can do—for we dare not meet a powerful challenge at odds and split asunder.

To those new States whom we welcome to the ranks of the free, we pledge our word that one form of colonial control shall not have passed away merely to be replaced by a far more iron tyranny. We shall not always expect to find them supporting our view. But we shall always hope to find them strongly supporting their own freedom—and to remember that, in the past, those who foolishly sought power by riding the back of the tiger ended up inside. [laughter and applause]

To those people in the huts and villages of half the globe struggling to break the bonds of mass misery, we pledge our best effort to help them help themselves, for whatever period is required—not because the communists may be doing it, not because we seek their votes, but because it is right. If a free society cannot help the many who are poor, it cannot save the few who are rich. [applause]

To our sister republics south of our border, we offer a special pledge—to convert our good words into good deeds—in a new alliance for progress—to assist free men and free governments in casting off the chains of poverty. But this peaceful revolution of hope cannot become the prey of hostile powers. Let all our neighbors know that we shall join with them to oppose aggression or subversion anywhere in the Americas. And let every other power know that this Hemisphere intends to remain the master of its own house.

To that world assembly of sovereign states, the United Nations, our last best hope in an age where the instruments of war have far outpaced the instruments of peace, we renew our pledge of support—to prevent it from becoming merely a forum for invective—to strengthen its shield of the new and the weak—and to enlarge the area in which its writ may run.

Finally, to those nations who would make themselves our adversary, we offer not a pledge but a request: that both sides begin anew the quest for peace, before the dark powers of destruction unleashed by science engulf all humanity in planned or accidental self-destruction.

We dare not tempt them with weakness. For only when our arms are sufficient beyond doubt can we be certain beyond doubt that they will never be employed.

But neither can two great and powerful groups of nations take comfort from our present course—both sides overburdened by the cost of modern weapons, both rightly alarmed by the steady spread of the deadly atom, both racing to alter that uncertain balance of terror that stays the hand of mankind's final war.

So let us begin anew—remembering on both sides that civility is not a sign of weakness, and sincerity is always subject to proof. Let us never negotiate out of fear. But let us never fear to negotiate. [applause]

Let both sides explore what problems unite us instead of belaboring those problems which divide us.

Let both sides, for the first time, formulate serious and precise proposals for the inspection and control of arms—and bring

the absolute power to destroy other nations under the absolute control of all nations. [brief applause]

Let both sides seek to invoke the wonders of science instead of its terrors. Together let us explore the stars, conquer the deserts, eradicate disease, tap the ocean depths, and encourage the arts and commerce.

Let both sides unite to heed in all corners of the earth the command of Isaiah—to "undo the heavy burdens . . . (and) let the oppressed go free."

And if a beachhead of cooperation may push back the jungle of suspicion, let both sides join in creating a new endeavor, not a new balance of power, but a new world of law, where the strong are just and the weak secure and the peace preserved.

All this will not be finished in the first 100 days. Nor will it be finished in the first 1,000 days, nor in the life of this Administration, nor even perhaps in our lifetime on this planet. But let us begin. [applause]

In your hands, my fellow citizens, more than mine, will rest the final success or failure of our course. Since this country was founded, each generation of Americans has been summoned to give testimony to its national loyalty. The graves of young Americans who answered the call to service surround the globe.

Now the trumpet summons us again—not as a call to bear arms, though arms we need; not as a call to battle, though embattled we are—but a call to bear the burden of a long twilight struggle, year in and year out, "rejoicing in hope, patient in tribulation"—a struggle against the common enemies of man: tyranny, poverty, disease, and war itself.

Can we forge against these enemies a grand and global alliance, North and South, East and West, that can assure a more fruitful life for all mankind? Will you join in that historic effort? [cheers and applause]

In the long history of the world, only a few generations have been granted the role of defending freedom in its hour of maximum danger. I do not shrink from this responsibility—I welcome it. [applause] I do not believe that any of us would exchange places with any other people or any other generation. The energy, the faith, the devotion which we bring to this endeavor will light our country and all who serve it—and the glow from that fire can truly light the world.

And so, my fellow Americans: ask not what your country can do for you—ask what you can do for your country. [applause]

My fellow citizens of the world: ask not what America will do for you, but what together we can do for the freedom of man. [brief applause]

Finally, whether you are citizens of America or citizens of the world, ask of us here the same high standards of strength and sacrifice which we ask of you. With a good conscience our only sure reward, with history the final judge of our deeds, let us go forth to lead the land we love, asking His blessing and His help, but knowing that here on earth God's work must truly be our own. [sustained applause]

Kennedy's "Memorabilia" Version of the Address, January 17, 1961

[Note: The nine-page handwritten document transcribed below is barely legible in many places, and very rough. John F. Kennedy's handwriting circa 1961 was often difficult to decipher in the best of circumstances, and this document was written in flight. None of those who were most intimately familiar with Kennedy's handwriting are available today to verify this version; while the acknowledgments gratefully note much assistance, responsibility for this nearly complete transcription lies with the author. Words clearly crossed out, even if legible, have been omitted from this transcription. But others that seem to represent incomplete thoughts, or only partial editing, are included, with those that appear duplicative or intended to be stricken in brackets. The punctuation is also rough. In short, this was never intended to be seen as anything other than a draft.]

An inaugural is an end as well as a beginning. Today I am linked with all the 35 other presidents and three of whom are with us today [and 3 of whom are with us here], and all those other men who stood in this same place, took the same oath, made the same commitment to the preservation of the American constitution and its promises that I have made today.

We are a young people—in an old Republic. But though we are old—at least as the life of political systems are measured, we must not that forget that we are descended from revolutionaries—I stand in succession to 5 men, Washington, Adams, Jefferson, Madison & Monroe, who participated in a revolution more drastic and far-reaching than any which now shapes the world. And though time may have legitimized our revolutionary predictions which they are founded remain today as challenging as it was nearly two centuries ago—the concept that the rights we enjoy come not from the generosity of the state but the hand of God.

I hope that the word will go out from this place today to a watching world that a new generation of Americans—born in this century—disciplined by war—have come to positions of responsibility here in the Sixties.

And I hope friends and foe alike [Republic] will understand that we have not come to power in order to participate in or countenance the defeat of the revolutionary concepts to which this country has always been committed and which are now at issue in the world struggle.

The principles for which our own ancestors fought here, we fight for around the globe. And we shall pay any price, bear any burden—meet any hardship, support any friend—oppose any foe—to that end we [———] in the this rich heritage.

In this crucial decade of the '60's may well be determined the success or failure of our course. We set sail today on a sea stirred by subterranean explosions—by currents which, twisting and turning, threatening to engulf us by horizons lit by the crackle of strife and division.

But we sail with high confidence in the fixed stars that have guided us to our present power—the desire for peace—but peace with freedom—the desire for prosperity—but a prosperity in which others share—the belief in our God—but with respect for the belief of others. In short we seek the circumstances which make peace for ourselves & for others and for all children the precepts of the just life.

In your hands, my fellow citizens more than mine, lie the final answer. Since this country was founded each generation of Americans has been called at least once to give testimony to their national loyalty. The graves of young Americans who answered the call circle the globe.

Now we must decide whether once again Americans are ready to pay the price of maintaining their freedom. Hopefully the price may not be the sharp sacrifice of war—but rather we must be ready to patiently bear burdens year in and year out in order to win the twilight war of our day.

Today we sound the trumpet again, not as a call to arms, though arms we need—not [———] a call to battle, though embattled we are. But a call a broader, more basic struggle against the common enemies of man—tyranny, poverty, disease, and war itself.

Can we forge against these enemies, a grand alliance North & South—East & West—that can insure a more fruitful life for all mankind—Will you join in that historic struggle. To few generations has it been given—in the long history of the world—to have a chance, by events and will, to be the chief defender of freedom at a time of maximum danger. I do not shrink from this responsibility—I welcome it—I do not believe we would change places with any other people of any other generation—The energy, faith, compliance and devotion to the cause of freedom will light this country and those around the world who stand on the knife edge of decision. We hold out to them our hand.

My fellow Americans, ask not what your country is going to do for you—ask what you can do for your country—My fellow citizens of the world, ask not what America or others will do for you—Ask rather what you [give for] can do for freedom. Ask of us the same high standards of sacrifice and strength of heart and soul that we seek from you.

Theodore Sorensen's Draft Inaugural Parody, January 17, 1962

[Passages substantially as delivered by JFK at the Democratic National Committee dinner, January 20, 1962, are in italics.]

We observe tonight not a celebration of freedom but a victory of party—urging renewal instead of change. *For we are sworn to pay off the same party debt our forebears ran up nearly a year and three months ago.*

But let every Republican know, whether he wishes us well or ill, that we shall pay any price, bear any burden, meet any hardship, support any friend, oppose any foe to assure the survival and the success of our Party.

This much we pledge—and (I hope) much more.

To those old contributors whose charitable and financial grace we covet, we pledge the loyalty of grateful friends. Well-heeled, there is little we cannot do in a host of Congressional campaigns. Impoverished, there is little we can do—for we dare not meet a powerful challenge in debt and short of credit.

To those new voters whom we welcome to the ranks of the party, we pledge our word that one form of parental control shall not have passed away merely to be replaced by another father image. We shall not always expect to find them supporting our candidates. But we shall always hope to find them strongly supporting their own future—and to remember that, in the past, those who foolishly sought power by riding the back of the elephant ended up without patronage.

To our brother Democrats south of the Mason-Dixon line, we offer a new "Alliance for Progress": Kennedy and Johnson.

To our candidates for that worldly assembly of fifty states, the Congress, we renew our pledge of support—to prevent it from becoming merely a forum for G.O.P. invective—to maintain its chairmanships in Democratic hands—and to enlarge the area in which our members sit. We dare not neglect our own majorities. For only when we have the votes sufficient beyond doubt can we be certain beyond doubt that they will never be needed in a roll-call.

Finally, to those politicians who would make themselves our adversary, we offer not a pledge but a request: that both sides begin anew the quest for Federal funds. For two great and powerful parties cannot take comfort from the facts of current political life: both sides over-burdened by the cost of modern elections, both rightly alarmed by the steady spread of their deficits, yet both racing to alter the size and shape of uncertain Congressional districts.

Our deficit will not be paid off in the next one hundred days. Nor will it be paid off in the first one thousand days, nor in the life of this Administration, nor even perhaps in our lifetime on this planet. But let us begin—remembering that generosity is not a sign of weakness and that ambassadors are always subject to [Senate] confirmation. For if the Democratic Party cannot be helped by the many who are poor, it cannot be saved by the few who are rich.

In your hands, my fellow Democrats, more than mine, will rest the final success or failure of our course. Since this party was founded, each generation of Democrats has been summoned to give money to its national treasury.

Now the Chairman summons us again—not as a call to cast votes, though votes we need—not as a call to man the polls, though polls we are taking—but a call to bear the financial burden of a long political struggle, year in and year out—a struggle against the common enemies of all Democrats: Miller, Goldwater, Rockefeller, and Nixon himself.

Can we forge against these enemies a united and prosperous party, North and South, East and West? Will you join in that pecuniary effort?

I do not believe that any of us would exchange places with any other party or any other Administration. The checks, the cash, the notes which we bring to this endeavor will light our party and all who serve it—and the smoke from that fire can truly smother the Republicans.

And so, my fellow Democrats: Ask not what your party can give to you—ask what you can give to your party.

Let us never contribute to our own decline. But let us never decline a contribution.

Acknowledgments

THIS IS my third book, but my first based to any significant degree on interviews. So I must begin these acknowledgments by thanking a number of people for their generosity with their time and thoughts: Ben Bradlee; Professor Suheil Bushrui, director of the Kahil Gibran Research and Studies Project of the University of Maryland's Center for International Development and Conflict Management; Myer Feldman; Professor John Kenneth Galbraith; William Lee Miller of the University of Virginia's Miller Center of Public Affairs; Professor Arthur Schlesinger, Jr.; and Senator Harris Wofford. Peter Kann, dear friend and former boss, gave me invaluable suggestions on how to approach one key interview.

That interview—and each of the conversations that form the heart of the original material in this book—was with Theodore C. Sorensen. This book would not have been worthwhile without Ted Sorensen's cooperation. I think it is important for me to acknowledge this fact, simply and clearly; I know that some may say it has colored the analysis, though I do not believe that to be the case.

The documentary record establishes that the circumstances surrounding the making of President Kennedy's inaugural address were truly known only to two men; of them, only Ted Sorensen survives. He has never before answered questions about the writing of the address in any detail. In fact, many of Sorensen's answers to such questions had, over the years, taken on a stock quality. That he finally agreed to go beyond this is a great gift to history, and I hope I have made the most of it. But whatever conclusion readers reach, I am forever indebted to Ted Sorensen for his courtesy, his professionalism, and his patience. Ditto for Ted's enormously capable assistant, Laurie Morris.

For help in assembling research materials, I owe thanks to the entire reference staff of the John Fitzgerald Kennedy Library, but especially to reference archivist Stephen Plotkin, who met repeated requests with efficiency, intelligence, and good cheer. Other important assistance in locating research materials was provided by Sylvia Baldwin of Professor Galbraith's office at Harvard; Don Graham of the Washington Post Company and George J. Gillespie, III, Esq., on behalf of the Estate of Katharine Graham and the papers of Philip Graham; Professor James Goodman of Rutgers University; Diane Kaplan of the Yale University Library; Muriel Keys of the *Antioch Review*; Alexis Luckey of the Miller Center; Charlotte Murphy of the Choate school; Professor Vito Silvestri; and the staff of the Library of Congress Photoduplication Service, especially senior search examiner Bonnie Coles.

As always, research sometimes fails to yield results. In this case I tried to locate drafts of the Kennedy inaugural written by Allan Nevins and Joseph Kraft but could not do so. I now believe both drafts to be lost. That said, I greatly appreciate help I received in trying to find these documents from Professor Nevins's daughter, Meredith Mayer, and his granddaughter, my friend and former colleague Jane Mayer, and from Mr. Kraft's widow, Polly Kraft Cutler, and her husband, Lloyd Cutler.

Two key documents I did locate needed deciphering. For invaluable assistance in interpreting Evelyn Lincoln's shorthand and creating Appendix C, I thank three very talented executive assistants, Connie De Maria of Tofel & Partners, LLP, and Olga Lisofski and Mary Lou Dumenico of Dow Jones & Company. For crucial help in reading President Kennedy's handwriting and creating Appendix F, I am indebted to two outstanding veterans of the Kennedy White House, Gloria Sitrin and Helen Westbrook, and another person with substantial experience in reading the president's handwriting whose identity I promised to protect in this context. It is particularly important to say with respect to these appendices that they remain imprecise, and that the responsibility for any errors in them, or elsewhere here, is mine alone.

The manuscript for this book was improved by readings of it undertaken by a number of friends. These included Gail and Walter Harris, who provided a close and perceptive review, and an important change in the preface, and David Stone, who not only put me in touch with his former boss, Harris Wofford, but also later provided a very thoughtful reading. Don Baer, who played a key role in the writing of the 1997 Clinton inaugural address, and Ray Price, who took the lead in writing the 1969 and 1973 Nixon inaugurals, both read the manuscript and offered valuable insights and much-treasured support.

Ivan Dee was enthusiastic about this book from the first, and steadfast in his commitment even when another author surprised us both by having chosen the same subject. Jim Friedlich, friend, former colleague, and budding media mogul, wisely urged the inclusion of a DVD of the speech.

This book is dedicated to Professor Richard E. Neustadt. Dick Neustadt's *Presidential Power* intrigued and influenced John Kennedy, and Dick and his work make a few appearances in these pages. I first encountered *Presidential Power* in high school, and immediately devoured it. It was then my great good fortune to meet Dick in a graduate-level seminar at Harvard. Undaunted by being the only college junior in the classroom, I thoroughly dominated the discussion, eagerly contending with doctoral students and the instructor himself. Many professors would have tossed me out; this one marched across the room as soon as the first session was over, stuck out his hand, and said, "I'm Dick Neustadt. That was really fun." It became the best class I ever took, and he was the best teacher I ever had. I was later a teaching assistant for him, an academic advisee of his, and, finally, a friend of twenty years. We chatted endlessly, mirthfully, and mostly about the presidency.

Just after I began work on this book, in late October 2003, I arranged to have dinner with Dick during a business trip of mine to London, where he had come to live most of the time. I waited until dinner to tell him about the book; I felt confident he'd get a big kick out of it. But on a Monday evening Dick had to cancel dinner, and by Friday night he had died, aged eighty-five. I miss him terribly.

Finally, it's again my great good fortune to be able to acknowledge my family. My father, Robert L. Tofel, voted for Nixon over Kennedy, but has since converted to become an even more ardent Democrat than I am. His commitment and love continues to ease any task I undertake. One of my own earliest memories of President Kennedy dates to November 22, 1963, and involves my mother, Carol Collins Tofel. Like many children my age—I was six—I first glimpsed the magnitude of that day's loss in the reaction of a parent. My mother, driving my brother and I to our weekly family dinner with her parents, was so overcome by grief that she had to pull our car off the road. I still remember the precise point on New York's West Side Highway where this took place; I have been trying ever since to understand what so deeply moved her. Even more than sixteen years after her own death I have felt her support in this effort, as in everything I do.

My wife, Jeanne Straus, remains my first editor and best friend. Of my three books, this is the first whose subject truly engaged her, and she was therefore of even greater help in shaping the text than she has been previously. Similarly, this is the first of my books to really absorb our daughter, Rachel Straus Tofel, and it has gained as well from her suggestions. Our son, Colin Straus Tofel, promises to read the book someday, but he has already contributed immeasurably, along with his mother and sister, in filling the home in which it was written with love and laughter. In writing, as in everything, that makes all the difference.

R. J. T.

Riverdale, New York
March 2005

Sources

Patrick Anderson, *The President's Men: White House Assistants of Franklin D. Roosevelt, Harry S Truman, Dwight D. Eisenhower, John F. Kennedy and Lyndon B. Johnson.* Garden City, N.Y., Doubleday, 1968.

Max Ascoli, "The Inaugural Address," *The Reporter*, February 2, 1961, p. 10.

U. E. Baughman with Leonard Robinson, *Secret Service Chief.* New York, Harper and Row, 1962.

Robert Bellah, "Civil Religion in America," *Daedalus*, vol. 96, no. 1 (Winter 1967), p. 1.

Paul Boller, Jr., *Presidential Inaugurations.* New York, Harcourt, 2001.

Daniel Boorstin, "Our Only American Ritual," *U.S. News & World Report*, January 30, 1989, p. 35.

Laura Bergquist, *A Very Special President.* New York, McGraw-Hill, 1965.

Joan and Clay Blair, Jr., *The Search for JFK.* New York, Berkley, 1976.

Benjamin Bradlee, *Conversations with Kennedy.* New York, W. W. Norton, 1975.

Carl Brauer, *Presidential Transitions: Eisenhower Through Reagan.* New York, Oxford University Press, 1986.

John Buchan (Lord Tweedsmuir), *Pilgrim's Way: An Essay in Recollection.* Cambridge, Mass., Houghton Mifflin, 1940.

James MacGregor Burns, *John Kennedy: A Political Profile.* New York, Harcourt, Brace, 1960.

Karlyn Kohrs Campbell and Kathleen Hall Jamieson, *Deeds Done in Words: Presidential Rhetoric and the Genres of Governance.* Chicago, University of Chicago Press, 1990.

William Carleton, "Kennedy in History: An Early Appraisal," *Antioch Review,* vol. 24 (Fall 1964), p. 277.

Douglass Cater, "Max Ascoli, of *The Reporter,*" *Encounter,* vol. L, no. 4 (March 1978), p. 49.

Winston Churchill, *Great Contemporaries.* Rev. ed., London, Macmillan, 1942; reprint, Safety Harbor, Fla., Simon Publications, 2001.

———, ed., *Never Give In! The Best of Winston's Churchill's Speeches.* New York Hyperion, 2003.

———, *While England Slept: A Survey of World Affairs 1932–1938.* New York, G. P. Putnam's Sons, 1938.

Thurston Clarke, *Ask Not: The Inauguration of John F. Kennedy and the Speech That Changed America.* New York, Henry Holt, 2004.

Robert Dallek, *An Unfinished Life: John F. Kennedy, 1917–1963.* Boston, Little, Brown, 2003.

Nancy Dickerson, *Among Those Present: A Reporter's View of Twenty-Five Years in Washington.* New York, Random House, 1976; Ballantine paperback, 1977.

Dwight Eisenhower, *Waging Peace: The White House Years, 1956–1961.* Garden City, N.Y., Doubleday, 1965.

Harold Faber, ed., *The Kennedy Years* [from *The New York Times*]. New York, Viking Press, 1964.

Henry Fairlie, *The Kennedy Promise: The Politics of Expectation.* Garden City, N.Y., Doubleday, 1973.

John Kenneth Galbraith, *A Life in Our Times: Memoirs.* Boston, Houghton Mifflin, 1981.

———, *Ambassador's Journal: A Personal Account of the Kennedy Years.* Boston, Houghton Mifflin, 1969.

——— (James Goodman, ed.), *Letters to Kennedy.* Cambridge, Mass., Harvard University Press, 1998.

Mary Gallagher (Frances Leighton, ed.), *My Life with Jacqueline Kennedy.* New York, David McKay, 1969.

James Golden, "John F. Kennedy and the 'Ghosts,'" *Quarterly Journal of Speech,* vol. LII, no. 4 (December 1966), p. 348.

Steven Goldzwig and George Dionisopoulos, *"In a Perilous Hour": The Public Address of John F. Kennedy*. Westport, Conn., Greenwood Press, 1995.

Doris Kearns Goodwin, *The Fitzgeralds and the Kennedys*. New York, Simon and Schuster, 1987.

Katharine Graham, *Personal History*. New York, Alfred A. Knopf, 1997.

Richard Grossman, ed., *Let Us Begin: The First 100 Days of the Kennedy Administration*. New York, Simon and Schuster, 1961.

Nigel Hamilton, *JFK: Reckless Youth*. New York, Random House, 1992.

Paul R. Henggeler, *The Kennedy Persuasion: The Politics of Style Since JFK*. Chicago, Ivan R. Dee, 1995.

C. David Heymann, *A Woman Named Jackie*. New York, Carol Communications, 1989.

Inaugural Addresses of the Presidents of the United States. 2 vols., Bedford, Mass., Applewood, 2001.

Charles Jones, ed., *Preparing to Be President: The Memos of Richard E. Neustadt*. Washington, D.C., AEI Press, 2000.

John F. Kennedy, *Profiles in Courage*. New York, Harper and Brothers, 1956.

——— (Allan Nevins, ed.), *The Strategy of Peace*. New York, Harper and Brothers, 1960; Popular Library paperback, 1961.

———, *Why England Slept*. New York, Wilfred Funk, 1940.

Rose Kennedy, *Times to Remember*. Garden City, N.Y., Doubleday, 1974.

Edward Kenny, "Another Look at Kennedy's Inaugural Address," *Today's Speech*, vol. 13, no. 4 (November 1965), p. 17.

Lincoln Kirstein, "The New Augustan Age," *The Nation*, February 4, 1961, pp. 106–108.

Fletcher Knebel, "Pulitzer Prize Entry: John F. Kennedy," in Eric Sevareid, ed., *Candidates 1960: Behind the Headlines in the Presidential Race*. New York, Basic Books, 1959.

Evelyn Lincoln, *My Twelve Years with John F. Kennedy*. New York, David McKay, 1965.

William Manchester, *One Brief Shining Moment: Remembering Kennedy*. Boston, Little, Brown, 1983.

———, *Portrait of a President: John F. Kennedy in Profile*. Rev. ed., Boston, Little, Brown, 1967.

Ralph Martin, *A Hero for Our Time: An Intimate Story of the Kennedy Years*. New York, Macmillan, 1983.

——— and Ed Plaut, *Front Runner, Dark Horse*. Garden City, N.Y., Doubleday, 1960.

Christopher Matthews, *Kennedy and Nixon: The Rivalry That Shaped Postwar America*. New York, Simon and Schuster, 1996.

Michael Medved, *The Shadow Presidents: The Secret History of the Chief Executives and Their Top Aides*. New York, Times Books, 1979.

William Lee Miller, "Ted Sorensen of Nebraska," *The Reporter*, February 13, 1964, pp. 24–27.

Kenneth O'Donnell and David Powers, with Joe McCarthy, *"Johnny, We Hardly Knew Ye": Memories of John Fitzgerald Kennedy*. Boston, Little, Brown, 1970.

Stan Opotowsky, *The Kennedy Government*. New York, E. P. Dutton, 1961.

Leonard Osborne, "Rhetorical Patterns in President Kennedy's Major Speeches," *Presidential Studies Quarterly*, vol. X (Summer 1980), p. 332.

Herbert Parmet, *Jack: The Struggles of John F. Kennedy*. New York, Dial Press, 1980.

———, *JFK: The Presidency of John F. Kennedy*. New York, Dial Press, 1983.

Geoffrey Perrett, *Jack: A Life Like No Other*. New York, Random House, 2001.

Public Papers of the Presidents of the United States: John F. Kennedy 1961. Washington, D.C., U.S. Government Printing Office, 1962.

Richard Reeves, *President Kennedy: Profile of Power*. New York, Simon and Schuster, 1993.

Halford Ryan, *American Rhetoric from Roosevelt to Reagan*. Prospect Heights, Ill., Waveland Press, 1983.

William Safire, *Safire's New Political Dictionary: The Definitive Guide to the New Language of Politics*. New York, Random House, 1993.

Pierre Salinger, *With Kennedy*. Garden City, N.Y., Doubleday, 1966.

Arthur Schlesinger, Jr., *A Thousand Days: John F. Kennedy in the White House*. Boston, Houghton Mifflin, 1965.

————, *Kennedy or Nixon: Does It Make Any Difference?* New York, Macmillan, 1960.

Hugh Sidey, *John F. Kennedy, President: A Reporter's Inside Story.* New York, Atheneum, 1963.

Vito Silvestri, *Becoming JFK: A Profile in Communication.* Westport, Conn., Praeger, 2000.

Sally Bedell Smith, *Grace and Power: The Private World of the Kennedy White House.* New York, Random House, 2004.

Theodore Sorensen, *Decision-Making in the White House: The Olive Branch or the Arrows.* New York, Columbia University Press, 1963.

————, *Kennedy.* New York, Harper and Row, 1965.

————, *The Kennedy Legacy.* New York, Macmillan, 1969.

————, ed., *"Let the Word Go Forth": The Speeches, Statements, and Writings of John F. Kennedy, 1947 to 1963.* New York, Delacorte Press, 1988.

Speeches, Remarks and Statements of Senator John F. Kennedy, August 1 Through November 7, 1960. Washington, D.C., U.S. Government Printing Office, 1961.

Gerald and Deborah Strober, *"Let Us Begin Anew": An Oral History of the Kennedy Presidency.* New York, HarperCollins, 1993.

William Strunk, Jr., and E. B. White, *The Elements of Style.* New York, Macmillan, 1959.

Lester Tanzer, ed., *The Kennedy Circle.* Washington, D.C., Luce, 1961.

James Taranto and Leonard Leo, eds., *Presidential Leadership: Rating the Best and the Worst in the White House.* New York, Wall Street Journal Books, 2004.

Maxwell Taylor, *The Uncertain Trumpet.* New York, Harper and Brothers, 1960.

Jack Valenti, *Speak Up with Confidence: How to Prepare, Learn, and Deliver Effective Speeches.* New York, Hyperion, 2002.

Ronald C. White, Jr., *Lincoln's Greatest Speech: The Second Inaugural.* New York, Simon and Schuster, 2002.

————, *The Eloquent President: A Portrait of Lincoln Through His Words.* New York, Random House, 2005.

Theodore H. White, *The Making of the President 1960.* New York, Atheneum, 1961.

Tom Wicker, *Kennedy Without Tears: The Man Behind the Myth.* New York, William Morrow, 1964.

Garry Wills, *Lincoln at Gettysburg: The Words That Remade America.* New York, Simon and Schuster, 1992.

Theodore Windt and Beth Ingold, *Essays in Presidential Rhetoric, Second Edition.* Dubuque, Ia., Kendall/Hunt, 1987.

Theodore Windt, Jr., "President John F. Kennedy's Inaugural Address, 1961" in Halford Ryan, ed., *The Inaugural Addresses of Twentieth Century American Presidents.* Westport, Conn., Praeger, 1993.

Harris Wofford, *Of Kennedys and Kings: Making Sense of the Sixties.* New York, Farrar Straus and Giroux, 1980.

Donald Wolfarth, "John F. Kennedy in the Tradition of Inaugural Speeches," *Quarterly Journal of Speech*, vol. XLVII (April 1961), p. 124.

Notes

REFERENCES to authors, unless otherwise indicated, are to their books and articles listed under Sources.

Abbreviations

Campaign	*The Speeches, Remarks, Press Conferences, and Statements of Senator John F. Kennedy, August 1 Through November 7, 1960* (U.S. Government Printing Office, Washington, D.C., 1961)
FRUS	*Foreign Relations of the United States, 1961–1963*
JFKL	John F. Kennedy Library
NYHT	*New York Herald Tribune*
NYT	*New York Times*
OH	oral history
POF	President's Office Files (JFKL)
PPP	*Public Papers of the President, John F. Kennedy*
WP	*Washington Post*
WS	*Washington Star*
TCSF	Theodore Sorensen Files (JFKL)
WHCF	White House Central Files (JFKL)
WHCSF	White House Central Special Files (JFKL)

page

5   Kennedy's early morning: Lincoln diary for 1/20/61, Lincoln papers, Box 4, folder 2, JFKL; Lincoln at 224–225.

6   Kennedy had opted for additional steroids: See Dallek at 275.

6   He may have taken Dexedrine: Perrett at 279.

7   green paint and "Roost-No-More": *Time*, January 27, 1961, at 8–9.

7   Hoover brokered the meeting: Matthews at 184.

7   final night in the shelter: Eisenhower at 617.

7   Graham dinner party: Graham at 272–273.

8   "You two are living like Presidents": O'Donnell and Powers at 278.

8   "It's better than mine": *ibid.* at 278. Martin at 8 says it was Jefferson's second inaugural address to which Kennedy made the comparison, though Jefferson's first—"We are all Republicans, we are all Federalists"—is by far the better known speech. Clarke at 155–156 points out that the selections in the program from Jefferson did not include either inaugural.

9   "It will be a sensation": Sidey at 37.

9   "It's a smash": Salinger at 108.

9   left for the Capitol together: Boller at 92.

9n "There is always some bastard": Beschloss at 530n.

9   "Paddy the Irishman": Schlesinger, *A Thousand Days*, at 2.

11 dents in their pillboxes: Heymann at 256, 257n.

11 "the time hasn't come": Christopher Finan, *Alfred E. Smith: The Happy Warrior* (New York: Hill and Wang, 2002), at 230.

11 1956 Gallup poll: Burns at 235–236.

12 he had aides argue: Sorensen, *Kennedy*, at 82–83.

12 margin of victory: *ibid.* at 217–218.

12 outdoor inaugurations: Boorstin; Boller at 125–126.

13 three times in the snow: Boller at 65.

14 "not quite the independence to have it": Burns at 150–151.

14 "May I urge you to be patient?": Sorensen, *Kennedy*, at 151–152.

14 "and then takes his advice": Dallek at 260.

15 "he wasn't half as surprised": Dickerson at 67.

15 *The Longest Day*: O'Donnell and Powers at 280. Reeves at 35 and Brauer at 98 (citing Robert Kennedy OH in JFKL) say this conversation occurred on the ride to the Capitol, but the two men can be seen on film conversing during this awkward interlude, and the O'Donnell/Powers account thus seems likelier to be accurate.

15 "fairly far up": Sorensen interview, 2/12/04.

15 Sorensen background: Sorensen, *Kennedy*, at 12, 17.

15 he had still never been overseas: Sidey at 178; Sorensen interview, 9/1/04.

16 "my intellectual blood bank": Martin at 178.

16   "When Jack is wounded, Ted bleeds": Russell Baker, *NYT*, 1/22/61. The quote first appeared in a draft of an article Anthony Lewis wrote for the *New York Times Magazine*. Lewis sent the draft to Sorensen, and it appears in the latter's files in the JFKL.

16   "the power of words": Medved at 261.

16   "I never had anyone who could write for me": Matthews at 92.

16   "But it was not his": Sorensen, *Kennedy*, at 60.

16   "he tended to resent interlopers": Schlesinger, *A Thousand Days*, at 70.

17   "in a peculiarly impersonal way": Sorensen, *Kennedy*, at 263.

17   "as his equal": Medved at 268.

17   "Ted is such a little boy": Martin and Plaut at 255.

17   "more intimate and more separate": Beschloss at 127.

17   "'incredible' or 'incredulous'": Sorensen interview, 2/12/04.

17   "Cardinal Spellman is having to watch it on television": Galbraith, *A Life*, at 374.

18   Baughman summoned a fireman: Baughman at 3.

18   "You must have a hot speech": Parmet, *JFK*, at 4.

18   "an endless monotone": Fay at 92.

19   "her mahogany voice": Kirstein at 104.

19   "Let him read a poem": Smith at 62.

20n   as later published: Edward Connery Lathem, ed., *The Poetry of Robert Frost* (New York: Holt, Rinehart and Winston, 1969), at 422–425.

20   best remembered for its final lines: See, *e.g.*, Schlesinger, *A Thousand Days*, at 3.

20   not in the version he intended to read: See, *e.g.*, *WP*, 1/21/61 at A8; *WS*, 1/21/61 at A-5; *NYHT*, 1/21/61 at 4.

21   some days or weeks later: Frost used the phrases "Augustan age" and "poetry and power" as early as January 23. Kirstein at 108.

21   from Frost to Kennedy via Udall: See Udall to JFK, 3/1/61 in WHCSF, JFKL, Box 710.

22   he had donned thermal underwear: Dickerson at 67.

22   Fitzgerald's Bible: Goodwin at 809–810.

22   "without arousing the POAU": Sorensen, *Kennedy*, at 240.

23   "the portion of him most visible": Valenti at 33.

24   "His speeches were fact-filled": Burns at xiii.

24   "serious, sincere, slightly dull": Martin and Plaut at 216.

24   "nothing registered": Silvestri at 94–95, quoting Robert Healy.

24   Humphrey was the superior speaker. Cabell Phillips, *NYT Magazine*, 10/25/59 at 24, 48, and *passim*.

24   "I've got control": Silvestri at 94.

24   he had begun to slow his delivery: Silvestri at 95, quoting Mary McGrory.

24   "listening for the cadence and style": Martin at 180–181.

25   McClosky sat in the gallery: Silvestri at 96–97.

25   "a bit breathless and grim": Fletcher Knebel, "What You Don't Know About Kennedy," *Look*, 1/17/61 at 81.

26   original reading copy: POF, Box 34, Inaugural Address file, JFKL; Lincoln at 230–231.

26n Kennedy would have marked changes: Sorensen interviews, 1/21/04, 2/12/04.

26n Feldman concurs. Feldman interview, 7/21/04.

26   "somebody might have laughed": Sorensen interview, 2/12/04.

30   the most memorable portion: Galbraith, *Ambassador's Journal*, at 50–51.

30n Galbraith's attribution: Galbraith, *Letters to Kennedy*, at 136 n27.

30   his own most common grammatical error: Sorensen interview, 2/12/04.

31n "omit needless words": See Strunk at 17–19.

31n both believers in Strunk's rule: Sorensen interview, 2/12/04.

32   "If I have to hold both hands": Sorensen, *Kennedy*, at 180.

32   "distant cries of Yes, yes": *WP*, 1/21/61.

33   "I would do anything": Kirstein at 108.

38   "where a one-syllable word would do": Sorensen, *Kennedy*, at 240.

38   word counts: Undated U.S. Senate Memorandum in TCSF Inaugural Address Memoranda, etc., JFKL.

38   length of average inaugural address: *NYT*, 1/21/61.

38   Kennedy directed: Undated Sorensen handwritten legal pad notes in TCSF Inaugural Address Memoranda, etc., JFKL.

40   "no evidence of any editorial counsel": White, *Lincoln's Greatest Speech*, at 69.

40n assistance from Browning, Davis, and Blair: Boller at 144–145: White, *Eloquent President*, at 68.

40n Washington's address drafted by Madison: Boller. at 4.

40   "leave no copies around": Undated Sorensen handwritten legal pad notes, TCSF Inaugural Address Memoranda, etc., JFKL.

40   not even to Goodwin and Feldman: Sorensen interview, 12/18/03.

41   learned of his son's birth: Smith at 18–19; Parmet, *JFK*, at 70–71.

41   "a stream of thoughts": Feldman interview, 7/21/04.

41   some "early work": Sorensen interview, 9/1/04.

41 in no sense the "first draft": cf. Clarke at 26, citing only an interview with Feldman on this point.

41 Kennedy probably never saw the "treatment": Feldman interview, 7/21/04.

41 Sorensen did not show drafts to Feldman: Sorensen interview, 6/21/04.

41 did not begin drafting until much later: Sorensen interviews, 12/18/03, 2/12/04, 6/21/04.

42 Galbraith more interested in the Senate: Galbraith, *Ambassador's Journal*, at 1–2; Galbraith, *Letters to Kennedy*, at 15, 135–136 n26.

42 "period of penance": Sorensen, *Kennedy*, at 395.

42 "at a suitable distance": Galbraith, *A Life*, at 389.

42 Galbraith draft: The draft is found in the Galbraith Papers, WH files, Inaugural Address, 1st draft typescripts, JFKL.

43 "it wouldn't have taken a solicitation": Sorensen interview, 2/12/04.

43 "gold star membership in both groups": Galbraith to JFK, 11/17/60, Galbraith, *Letters to Kennedy*, at 34.

43 "it may not be vital": Galbraith e-mail to author, 4/9/04.

43 talked about the "tone and tenor": Lincoln memo for Silvestri, 3/2/87.

43 "changes [Kennedy] suggested": Galbraith to JFK, 1/9/61, Galbraith, *Letters to Kennedy*, at 15.

44 "essentially unfinished": Galbraith to JFK, 7/16/60, Galbraith, *Letters to Kennedy*, at 10–11.

44 "wasn't quite so close to Kennedy": Alan Otten, "What Do You Think, Ted?" [hereafter Otten] in Tanzer at 8, 19.

44 "a bird with a broken wing": Galbraith to JFK, 7/16/60, Galbraith, *Letters to Kennedy*, at 10–11.

45 "nonetheless qualities of its own": Schlesinger, *Kennedy or Nixon*, at 25.

45 had difficulty reading the text: Parmet, *JFK*, at 31.

45 after the general election campaign had restored his relationship: Otten in Tanzer at 8, 19–20.

45 "Ken is a towering figure in many ways": Sorensen interview, 2/12/04.

46 "Ted was there for the duration": Galbraith e-mail to author, 4/9/04.

47 Neustadt's transition advice: Neustadt to JFK, 9/15/60, in Jones at 35.

47 FDR first read Moley's draft: Kenneth Davis, *FDR: The New York Years 1928–1933* (New York: Random House, 1994), at 442–443.

47 "better get cracking": Sorensen interview, 2/12/04.

47 block wire: Block Wire, 12/23/60, TCSF Inaugural Address Memoranda, etc., JFKL.

48   Sorensen and Wofford selected speeches for publication: Parmet, *Jack*, at 486.

48n   "frontiers that are not geographic": Nevins to Sorensen, 7/8/60, in TCSF Campaign Files, Box 25, JFKL.

48n   Schlesinger March 1960 speech: Schlesinger, *A Thousand Days*, at 21.

48n   Sorensen who adopted the phrase: Sorensen interview, 9/1/04.

48n   others from whom drafts were solicited: See letters from Sorensen, 7/22/60, TCSF Campaign Files, Box 25, JFKL.

48   "I enjoy Nevins' reflections": JFK to Evan Thomas, 12/10/60, in Nevins correspondence for 1960, Nevins papers, Columbia University.

50   Stevenson confined himself to foreign policy: Box 47, folder 4, Stevenson Papers, Princeton University.

50   Dillon offered an outline and some notes: Clarke at 220n mistakenly attributes these notes, including a suggestion to address the "gold crisis," to Sorensen.

50   Sorensen recalls none: Sorensen interview, 12/18/03.

51   "reluctantly dipped into the file of phrases": Sorensen, *Kennedy*, at 234.

51   "using up some of our best lines": Sorensen interview, 1/21/04.

51   no inaugural draft had yet been written: Sorensen interview, 2/12/04.

52   "it would be hard to top": Sorensen, *Kennedy*, at 240–241.

52   probably on a legal pad: Sorensen always composed in longhand. Sorensen interview, 1/21/04.

53   "I know they don't": Sorensen interview, 12/18/03.

53   "I don't want to diminish him": *ibid.*

53   "some people think its words are holy": *ibid.*

54   "even if many of the words were written by Ted": Smith at 56.

54   "the underlying realities are similar": Sorensen interview, 1/21/04.

54   "my research associate": Kennedy, *Profiles*, at xviii.

54   book on New England's economic problems: Parmet, *Jack*, at 269–270.

55   "burdens of time and literary craftsmanship": *ibid.* at 333.

55   no draft was begun until after drafting the Massachusetts speech: Sorensen, *Kennedy*, at 240; Sorensen, interviews, 12/18/03, 2/12/04.

55   "TCS draft": Undated U.S. Senate Memorandum in TCSF Inaugural Address Memoranda, etc., JFKL.

55   "add style & eloquence": *ibid.*

56   a five-page document: POF, speech files, Inaugural Address, JFKL.

56   Sorensen is confident: Sorensen interview, 12/18/03.

56   "set a tone for the era about to begin": Sorensen, *Kennedy*, at 240.

58n "I hope you will read it carefully." TCSF, Inaugural Address Memoranda, etc., JFKL.

58n Clarke errs that draft is in TCSF: Clarke at 226n.

58n presumably also errs in stating as a fact that none was used: Clarke at 70.

58n Sorensen recalls a submission from Kraft. Sorensen interview, 1/21/04.

58n Kraft recalled: Kraft OH at 20, JFKL.

58n "I would have paid attention": Sorensen interview, 9/1/04.

58 Bowles/Rusk draft: Chester Bowles Papers, Box 216, folder 290, Yale University.

59 "He told me of his own potential following": Sorensen, *Kennedy*, at 150.

59 eight taken from Stevenson: The Stevenson draft is found in the Adlai Stevenson Papers, box 47, folder 4, Princeton University.

59 "like an unloved dog": Galbraith, *Ambassador's Journal*, at 16.

59 Galbraith's second draft: The draft is found in the Galbraith Papers, WH files, Inaugural Address, 2d draft typescripts, JFKL.

59 Galbraith's style was derivative of Stevenson's: Galbraith, *A Life*, at 292.

59 "no man can write another's prayers": Galbraith to JFK, 1/9/61, Galbraith, *Letters to Kennedy*, at 15–16.

60 Sorensen later listed guidelines: Sorensen, *Kennedy*, at 61–62.

60 "I am more orotund": *NYT*, 6/25/67.

60n Wofford speculates: Clarke at 70.

60n Galbraith and Stevenson did not confer directly: Galbraith e-mail to author, 7/27/04.

63n Graham offered a draft: Philip Graham to JFK, 1/5/61.

63n Vidal's suggestions: TCSF personal correpondence, box 84, JFKL.

65 "in every respect" Kennedy's own handiwork: Clarke at 93.

66 "group authorship is rarely, if ever, successful": Sorensen, *Decision-Making*, at 61–62.

67 the only extended telephone conversation Sorensen recalls: Sorensen interview, 2/12/04. Clarke, at 42, errs in saying that the brunch occurred at the home of Myer Feldman. Feldman notes that the party he hosted for the cabinet occurred after the inauguration. Feldman interview, 7/21/04.

67n Sorensen now insists it was outdoors: Sorensen interview, 12/18/03.

67n Mrs. Lincoln's book: Lincoln at 219–220.

67n Mrs. Lincoln's contemporaneous diaries: Lincoln Papers, box 4, folder 2, JFKL.

67n   the confusion likely began: Lincoln at 220.

67n   Lincoln diaries on JFK activities: Lincoln Papers, box 4, folder 2, JFKL.

68   "Ted Sorensen sat at a typewriter": Bergquist at 19. Sorensen, *Kennedy*, at 242, says he worked at the nearby Palm Beach Towers swimming pool. He may have started at Ambassador Kennedy's house and continued later at his hotel. He says he did not type this new draft.

68   Sorensen first labels it a "fraud": Sorensen interview, 12/18/03.

69   Kennedy's suggestion to Sorensen: Sorensen interviews, 12/18/03, 9/1/04. See also Sorensen, *Kennedy*, at 243, quoting Kennedy as saying, "An early draft of Roosevelt's Inaugural was discovered the other day— and brought $200,000 at an auction."

69   presented publicly as "an early draft of the inaugural speech": See, e.g., Charles Kenney, *John F. Kennedy, The Presidential Portfolio: History as Told Through the Collection of the John F. Kennedy Library and Museum* (New York: PublicAffairs, 2000), at 56–58.

70   "absolutely nothing to do with the evolution of the speech": Sorensen interview, 12/18/03.

70   Parmet on Kennedy's handwritten notes: Parmet, *Jack*, at 332.

70   "a charade, but an honorable one": Clarke at 93, 100, 102.

71   "Maybe he was doing it again": Sorensen interview, 9/1/04.

71   "The President's first draft of the inaugural address": Grossman, inside cover.

71   Sorensen reviewed draft with Lippmann: Lippmann OH at 6, JFKL.

72   "the famous Sorensen chiliastic turns of speech": *ibid.* If by chiliasm Lippmann meant the phrase "a thousand days," that was not Sorensen's. See text at 116–117.

72   Rusk suggestion: See Sorensen, *Kennedy*, at 243.

72   Clifford may have reviewed the draft: See Sorensen, *Kennedy* manuscript in TCSF, JFKL, at 8–18.

72   Galbraith's suggestions: See Galbraith, *Ambassador's Journal*, at 16; Galbraith, *Letters to Kennedy*, at 136 n27.

72   Kennedy had the reading copy with him: See Sorensen, *Kennedy*, at 243, though Sorensen there confuses the date of Kennedy's trip to New York.

72   hold-for-release version: TCSF, JFK speech files, Inaugural Address, Drafts & Press Releases, JFKL.

74   Wofford and Martin's roles: Wofford at 99; Wofford interview, 2/6/04. Clarke, at 135, adds Martin as Wofford's co-author, based on an interview Clarke conducted with Wofford; Wofford did not mention Martin to me.

74   Sorensen and what became Lincoln, NE, CORE chapter: *NYT Maga-zine*, 3/26/67.

74   Sorensen's testimony: Miller at 26.

74   Sorensen's first nationally published article: See Otten in Tanzer at 13.

74   conflicting accounts: Sorensen interview, 12/18/03; Clarke at 135–137; Wofford interview, 2/6/04.

77   "the issue of war and peace is involved": PPP, 1961, at 15–16.

77   "because they tend to divide": Fairlie at 260.

77   Rostow "generally credited": Sorensen interview, 9/1/04.

77   Kennedy had adopted Rostow's analysis: See, e.g., Kennedy, *Strategy of Peace*, at 77 (referring to "the process of economic take-off").

78   "the nature of the next stage": Rostow at 91.

78   "an adequately interesting and expensive outlet": *ibid*.

79   "exert its skill and strength": Quoted in Manchester, *Portrait*, at 125.

79   Rostow on the Soviets' choice: Rostow at 29, 119.

79   Rostow on the task for the West: *ibid*. at 105, 134, 164.

80   National Intelligence Estimate: FRUS, vol. V, Soviet Union.

81   "Mr. Khrushchev is in New York": Beschloss at 31.

81   Khrushchev's speech: See Dallek at 350.

81   "Communists are revolutionaries": Beschloss at 60.

81   National Intelligence Estimate: FRUS, vol. V, Soviet Union.

81   Khrushchev in English translation: *NYT*, 1/19/61.

82   *New York Times* editorial: *NYT*, 1/20/61.

82   "no reason why the United States should fear for its security": Fairlie at 24.

82   Kennedy on Chamberlain: Parmet, *Jack*, at 130.

82   *Why England Slept*: Kennedy, *Why*, at 107, 157.

83   "A democracy will merely try to counter-balance": *ibid*. at 106.

83   "*For the long run*": *ibid*. at 224 (emphasis in original).

83   "you cannot get voluntary action": *ibid*. at 161.

83   "In America that force is the presidency": Knebel at 187.

84   "JFK was very impressed": Sorensen interview, 9/1/04.

85   "expose the Great Fallacy": Taylor at 173.

85   "the sure notes of a certain trumpet": *ibid*. at 179–180.

86   "'the little book'": Strunk at vii.

86   "books with windswept tail fins and automatic verbs": *ibid*. at xii.

86   Strunk's "chief distinguishing mark": *ibid*. at xi.

86   may have received his copy from Kraft: Sorensen interview, 9/1/04.

86n   "erudition but not arrogance": Sorensen, *Kennedy*, at 62.

87   Strunk's watchwords: Strunk at 6, 14, 63, 67, 26, 17.

87   "not conscious of following the elaborate techniques": Sorensen, *Kennedy*, at 60–61.

88   the horse chestnut and the chestnut horse: Wills at 163.

88   "the lightning and the lightning bug": *ibid.*

88   Sorensen reading Pericles: Feldman interview, 7/21/04.

88   "I am sure JFK read it first": Sorensen interview, 9/1/04.

88   Pericles in Massachusetts speech: Sorensen, *Let the Word*, at 56.

89   Reeves on *While England Slept*: Reeves at 41, 668n.

89   beginning of *Why England Slept*: Kennedy, *Why*, at xxiii.

89   Reeves on *Great Contemporaries*: Reeves at 668n. Reeves may have this Churchill volume confused with another. The quoted sentence does not appear in the book, and the edition I have says it was first published in 1937, not 1922 as Reeves states.

90   not Churchill but Hemingway: Kennedy, *Profiles*, at 1.

90   Kennedy's "greatest admiration": Schlesinger, *A Thousand Days*, at 84.

93   "not a victory of party or of any class": Churchill, *Never Give In!*, at 391.

93   Kennedy copied and memorized Churchill: Fay at 173.

93   "both JFK and I loved Churchill": Sorensen interview, 1/21/04.

95   "We have a world capable of destroying itself": Hamilton at 748.

95   1958 address to Gridiron Club: JFK at Gridiron Club, 3/15/58, JFK Pre-Pres. Papers, box 900, JFKL.

95   Convention acceptance speech: Sorensen, *Let the Word*, at 99.

96   Kennedy's favorite "shorthand way": Sorensen interview, 1/21/04.

96   Taylor's final paragraph: Taylor at 179.

97   "The torch is a favorite political symbol": Safire at 808.

97   Nevins's introduction: Kennedy, *Strategy of Peace*, at xx.

97   "I think this Nation will rise to the test": Campaign at 298.

98   Kennedy provided much of the language for this paragraph: Sorensen interview, 1/21/04.

98n   first State of the Union: PPP, 1961, at 22–23.

99   Patrick Henry quote: See Campaign at 46, 1197 for uses of this quotation during the campaign.

99   "a deliberate rhythm": Valenti at 24.

100   an expression toward which Kennedy had been moving: Campaign at 53, 230.

101   Sorensen says Kennedy outlined approach: Sorensen interview, 1/21/04.

101   "sounded like a mining partnership": Sorensen, *Kennedy*, at 243.

101   "elimination of a mildly hectoring tone": Galbraith, *Ambassador's Journal*, at 16.

102   "It's a good line": Sorensen interview, 12/18/03.

103   tiger limerick: *NYT*, 1/21/61. Sorensen confirms this was the source. Sorensen interview, 1/21/04.

103   "Others differed": Galbraith, *Ambassador's Journal*, at 16.

103   "And the tigers are getting hungry": Clarke at 130.

103   Kennedy took note of Churchill's formulation: Martin and Plaut at 209.

104   "assuming it had a broader meaning": Sorensen, *Kennedy*, at 533.

104   "a musical ring": Sorensen interview, 1/21/04.

104   "we mistakenly dropped the 'el' ": Sorensen, *Kennedy*, at 533.

104   in the prepared text, but dropped on delivery: Compare Campaign at 1159–1166 (prepared text) with *ibid.* at 654–659 (speech as delivered).

104   *Kennedy* says words added by Kennedy himself: Sorensen, *Kennedy*, at 243.

105   Kennedy's remark to Bradlee: Bradlee at 152.

105   "We are in truth the last best hope on earth": Parmet, *Jack*, at 276.

106   Sorensen says Lincoln was source: Sorensen interview, 1/21/04.

106   "a symbol of all that we hope": Campaign at 231.

107   "many overlapping and conflicting roles": Sorensen, *Kennedy Legacy*, at 179.

107   Sorensen's belief on phrase: Sorensen interview, 1/21/04.

107   Sorensen hobby of writing doggerel: *ibid.*

107   Lincoln began with bad poetry: Wills at 149.

108   "it referred to human error": Sorensen speech at JFKL, 4/21/02, available on JFKL website.

109   "tells us more than 'Ask Not'": *ibid.*

109   "the most important sentence in the speech": Sorensen interview, 1/21/04.

109   "We must always keep our armaments equal to our commitments": Sorensen, *Kennedy*, at 602.

109   Kennedy quotes "iron curtain" speech: Campaign at 447.

109   Kennedy at Seattle: Campaign at 993–994.

109   "we will arm to disarm": Schlesinger, *Kennedy or Nixon*, at 42.

110n   first published no later than 1964: See *NYT*, 4/26/64.

110n   "it is beyond anything I've seen": Clarke at 206.

111   National Press Club Speech: The speech was delivered January 14, 1960. Sorensen, *Let the Word*, at 22.

111 "armed only with vague, speculative hopes": Kennedy, *Strategy of Peace*, at ix.

111 "we arm to parley": Campaign at 231, 241, 273, 352, 724.

111 Kennedy's favorite Churchill quote: Sorensen, *Kennedy*, at 602.

111 rooted in Dulles's snub of Zhou Enlai: Sorensen interview, 2/12/04.

112 "not what we fear separately but what we share together": Sorensen, *Let the Word*, at 39.

112 Sorensen says quotation was suggested by Rabbi Franck: Sorensen interview, 1/21/04.

113 "This got the message across": Sorensen interview, 2/12/04.

113 Lincoln only the second to quote the Bible: White, *Lincoln's Greatest Speech*, at 101.

113 "the inspiration of the inaugural address was religious": Fairlie at 109.

114 "the power of liturgy": See Fairlie at 109–110; Edward Corbett, "Analysis of the Style of John F. Kennedy's Inaugural Address," in Windt and Ingold at 101.

114 "essential to the rite of investiture": Campbell and Jamieson at 80.

115 "October is the month to prepare for action": Campaign at 576–577.

115 "Another 'Hundred Days'": Neustadt to JFK via Senator Henry Jackson, 9/15/60, Jones, ed., at 21–22.

115 Madison, WI, speech: Campaign at 713.

116 "irritated . . . by widespread press speculation": Sorensen, *Kennedy*, at 239.

116 Galbraith drafts: Galbraith first draft, JFKL, at 1–2; Galbraith second draft, JFKL, at 2.

116 "their finest hour": Churchill, *Never Give In!*, at 229.

117 Schlesinger contributed to at least one of Galbraith's drafts: Galbraith to JFK, 1/9/61, Galbraith, *Letters to Kennedy*, at 15.

117 Schlesinger does not recall: Schlesinger telephone conversation with author, 4/20/04.

117 "the sense of style": Galbraith e-mail to author, 4/9/04.

117 "a day or two later it was mildly historic": Galbraith, *Ambassador's Journal*, at 16.

118 "dictated as we discussed ideas": Sorensen, *Kennedy* manuscript at 8–19, JFKL.

119 Kennedy's allusions to Corinthians: See Martin and Plaut at 228; Campaign at 649, 809, 860, 914.

120 Gruening telegram: TCSF, JFK Speech Series, Inaugural Address, Memoranda, JFKL.

120 Sorensen agrees: Sorensen interview, 12/18/03.

122 New Testament quotations from Graham, Old from Franck: See Sorensen, *Kennedy*, at 240.

122 typed neatly on yellow paper: Sidey at 37.

122 "a noble and historic role": The speech was delivered January 2, 1960. Sorensen, *Let the Word*, at 90.

123n apparently one of the offerings from Graham: See Sidey at 36–37.

123n *Kennedy* says quotation was removed in-flight: Sorensen, *Kennedy*, at 243.

123n Kennedy pointed it out to Sidey: Sidey at 37.

124 Bartlett's: *Bartlett's Familiar Quotations*, 17th edition (Boston: Little, Brown, 2002), at 799. Kennedy used the Rousseau quote in a speech during his first race for Congress in 1946. Hamilton at 784.

124 Van Wyck Brooks quote: Schlesinger, *A Thousand Days*, at 4n.

124 Sorensen on Harding: Sorensen interview, 2/12/04.

125 published accounts credit Gibran: *e.g.*, Associated Press, 4/21/89.

125 Bushrui translation: Bushrui letter to author, 3/22/04.

125 Kennedy borrowed from Dr. St. John: *e.g.*, *Time*, 1/28/66.

125 "wishful thinking at best": Charlotte Murphy (director of communications, Choate Rosemary Hall) e-mail to author, 2/19/04.

126 change of *will* to *can*: Schlesinger, *A Thousand Days*, at 4, and Manchester, *One Brief Shining Moment*, at 128, both claiming that Kennedy made the change the previous day are incorrect.

127 "I say, 'Ask not.'" Sorensen interview, 2/12/04.

127 "Not that I loved Caesar less": Strunk at 14–15.

128 "the cause of all mankind is the cause of America": Campaign at 104, 114.

129 Harris draft: Harris to JFK, 1/14/61, JFKL.

129 Kennedy-Sorensen dialogue on peroration: Sorensen, *Kennedy*, at 243; Sorensen interview, 2/12/04.

129 effects of Sorensen's Unitarianism: Otten in Tanzer at 10–11; Sorensen interview, 2/12/04; Miller at 24–25.

135 Krock comparison with Wilson: Reeves at 41.

135 Lippmann evaluation: *NYHT*, 1/24/61.

135 Evans on Democrats' reactions: *NYHT*, 1/21/61.

135 *Wall Street Journal* editorial: 1/23/61.

135 Monroney and Alphand reactions: *NYT*, 1/21/61.

136 "Quotation of the Day": *ibid.*

136 *Time* comparison: 1/27/61.

136   Henry Wallace letter: Wallace to JFK, 1/22/61, WHCSF, box 913, JFKL.

136   White reaction: Schlesinger, *A Thousand Days*, at 732.

136   Steinbeck reaction: Steinbeck to JFK, 1/23/61, WHCSF, box 711.

136n   Kennedy's acknowledgment: JFK to Steinbeck, 1/31/61, WHCSF, box 913, JFKL.

137   Eleanor Roosevelt reaction: ER to JFK, 1/24/61, in Arthur Schlesinger Papers, box W-60, JFKL.

137   Walker's test: Richard Walker to JFK, 1/26/61, WHCF, JFKL.

137   Miss Alley's student: Joanne Kincaid to JFK, 3/27/61, WHCF, JFKL.

137n   Rosenthal and Sorensen on Cicero: Asher Rosenthal to JFK, 10/9/61, and Sorensen to Rosenthal, 11/20/61, WHCSF, JFKL.

137n   Wills comparison to Gorgias: Wills at 212.

138   Harris polling results: Harris report to JFK, 3/22/61, POF, box 105, JFKL.

138   Ascoli reaction to speech: Ascoli at 10.

139   Kennedy-Ascoli encounter: Cater at 49; author's conversation with William Lee Miller, former *Reporter* reporter, 10/27/04.

139   Reston reaction to speech: *NYT*, 1/22/61.

139   Max Lerner reaction: *New York Post*, 1/23/61.

139   Kennedy's UN speech: PPP, 1961, at 625, 626.

139   Kennedy's Seattle speech: PPP, 1961, at 472, 473.

140   Kennedy fund-raising dinner remarks: PPP, 1962, at 40–41.

141n   three names ending in "er": Sorensen interview, 1/21/04.

141   "it's sacrilege": *ibid.*

142   Ford dealer sign: Beschloss at 604.

144   memorial marker at Runnymede: *NYT*, 5/15/65.

144   Morison evaluation: Golden at 355, citing Morison's *Oxford History of the American People*, at 1111.

145   "his inaugural address in his own handwriting": *NYT*, 5/26/64.

145   "ask not" at auction: *NYT*, 3/26/71.

145n   Memorabilia version scrap at auction: Clarke at 107.

145   "more suited to the Stalinist era": Carleton at 291, 295.

145   McGovern's disillusionment: quoted in Strober at 483.

146   "It was brilliant; it was moving; it was dangerous": Fairlie at 102.

146   "they are offensive": *ibid.* at 105 (emphasis in original).

146   "Nixon's standard": quoted in Matthews at 271.

147   Nixon's second inaugural: Inaugural Addresses, vol. II, at 140–141.

148   Reagan in 1984: televised address to the nation, 5/9/84.

148   Dukakis in 1988: *WP*, 10/4/88.

148   "ask more of your candidates": *NYT*, 7/12/87.

148   Gephardt in Iowa: Associated Press, 9/18/87.

148   Biden quote: *NYT*, 7/12/87.

148   "the Bureau of Standards for Democrats": *ibid.*

148   Clinton's pilgrimage: Associated Press, 1/19/93.

148   Clinton at prayer breakfast: *Boston Globe*, 2/5/93.

148   observers on Bush: See, *e.g.*, Jim Hoagland, "Taking Up Kennedy's Torch," *WP*, 1/31/91.

149   Holbrooke in Bangkok: Holbrooke, *To End a War* (New York: Random House, 1998), at 44.

149   Mandela takes office: Associated Press, 5/10/94.

149   Netanyahu takes office: Associated Press, 6/18/96.

150   "Kennedy's symbolic stature": *USA Today*, 11/22/88.

150   polling data: The public opinion data summarized here is collected in the October/November 1998 issue of *The Public Perspective* at 10–11, and is part of the treasure trove preserved by the Roper Center at the University of Connecticut.

151   2004 Gallup survey: *Economist*, 6/26/04.

151   2003 nonpartisan survey: Taranto at 255–256.

151   "the most overrated president": *ibid.* at 259.

152   Noonan's view: *ibid.* at 168–169.

153   second-greatest speech in the history of television: *Boston Herald*, 8/29/00.

153   greatest American speeches of the twentieth century: *Richmond Times-Dispatch*, 6/25/03.

153   Sorensen's introduction: Sorensen, *Let the Word*, at 1.

Index

A NOTE ON THE AUTHOR

Richard J. Tofel is president and chief operating officer of the International Freedom Center, a newly organized museum and cultural center that will be built on the World Trade Center site in New York City. A graduate of Harvard College, Harvard Law School, and the John F. Kennedy School of Government at Harvard, Mr. Tofel formerly worked in a number of positions at Dow Jones & Company, including assistant publisher and, earlier, assistant managing editor of the *Wall Street Journal*. He has also written *Vanishing Point: The Disappearance of Judge Crater and the New York He Left Behind* and *A Legend in the Making*, an account of the New York Yankees in 1939, both widely praised. He lives with his wife and children in Riverdale, New York.